Taking Note:
From Poets' Notebooks

Edited by
Stephen Kuusisto, Deborah Tall,
and David Weiss

A Special Edition of Seneca Review

Hobart and William Smith Colleges Press, Geneva, New York, 1991

SENECA REVIEW   VOL. XXI, No. 2

Special Edition: Taking Note

EDITOR
Deborah Tall

CO-EDITORS FOR THIS ISSUE
Stephen Kuusisto and David Weiss

FOUNDING EDITORS
James Crenner
Ira Sadoff

CONTRIBUTING EDITORS
Donald Hall
Stephen Kuusisto
David Weiss

ASSISTANT EDITOR
Jennifer Corse Simon

CIRCULATION MANAGER
Sharon Elder

COVER DESIGN
Gwen Butler
(Marbled paper from the Rochester Folk Art Guild)

Seneca Review is published semi-annually by Hobart and William Smith Colleges, Geneva, NY 14456. Subscriptions are $8 per year, $15 for 2 years. Single copies of current or available back issues are $5 each.

Unsolicited manuscripts of poetry and criticism of contemporary poetry are read annually between September 1st and May 1st. Manuscripts sent at other times will be returned unread. No manuscripts can be returned unless accompanied by a stamped, self-addressed envelope.

Poems published in *Seneca Review* are indexed in *Index of American Periodical Verse, Annual Index to Poetry in Periodicals,* and *American Humanities Index.*

Library of Congress National Series Data Program ISSN 0037-2145.

Special edition, ISBN 0-934888-15-9

Copyright ⓡ 1991 by Hobart and William Smith Colleges.

Printed by Shipman Printing Industries, Niagara Falls, NY

CONTENTS

Introduction	5
Philip Booth	9
Sharon Bryan	15
Douglas Crase	23
Guy Davenport	29
Rita Dove	36
Stephen Dunn	44
Carolyn Forché	50
Reginald Gibbons	62
Allen Grossman	70
Donald Hall	75
Anselm Hollo	79
Garrett Hongo	86
Donald Justice	92
X.J. Kennedy	103
William Matthews	110
Mekeel McBride	118
J.D. McClatchy	125
Heather McHugh	137
Jane Miller	146
Robert Morgan	152
Lisel Mueller	158
Mary Oliver	164
Gregory Orr	172
Alicia Ostriker	178
Michael J. Rosen	184
Liz Rosenberg	191
Vern Rutsala	200
Peter Sacks	207
Laurie Sheck	219
William Stafford	226
Eleanor Ross Taylor	231
Rosanna Warren	239

The Note-Taking Habit

> It is a long time since I have kept any notes, taken any memoranda, written down my current reflections, taken a sheet of paper, as it were, into my confidence. Meanwhile so much has come and gone, so much that it is now too late to catch, to reproduce, to preserve. I have lost too much by losing, or rather by not having acquired, the note-taking habit.
>
> —Henry James

There are probably as many kinds of notebooks as poets who keep them. Called commonplace books, journals, diaries, they house under one cover lines of poetry, reflections, ideas, observations, feelings, quotations, impressions, confessions, aphorisms, sketches, speculations, intuitions, responses. "To catch, to reproduce, to preserve," writes James, nicely summarizing the impulse. In the verb "preserve," one feels the upstream swim against things passing; in "catch," that swipe at the will-o'-the-wisp of passing thought and sensation.

Notebooks, one also feels, register the effort to bring together those discrete dimensions of the writer's life—literary, biographical, intimate and mundane. Until I began to keep a notebook, I thought of myself as a writer only when I wrote; partly, I insisted on this distinction. To be father or son, someone who fixed cars, bought groceries, went to meetings, was something other, contiguous but discontinuous, immanent but shadowy. I would hardly think to recite a poem at the check-out counter or the bank, although each might find its place in a poem. "To imagine an American life," Robert Pinsky has written, "American poetry characteristically—maybe inevitably—begins by imagining, implicitly or explicitly, its own unrealized place in that life." To fuse those identities, poet and citizen, has been an enduring tension in American poetry since Whitman. In my case, to emerge from my basement study has been to squint and shake off the effects of hard concentration and odd, strong feelings and to move in a densely different atmosphere. When I was younger I turned the scribbled page face down on the desk and went off carrying my invisible identity into the world like a secret talisman. Yet it is hard not to feel a disability in what mends these gaps, bridging some of the inner dislocations which refigure the outer ones, carries one through fallow times.

A poem and the stuff of experience a poem draws on for its imagery are different things and of different orders. To paraphrase Stevens, a poem has a doubleness, a seeming subject and a true subject—like what happens when your eyes cross: the cat you are looking at splits in two—into apparent cat and central cat, the literal and the symbolic, the image of the cat and the language of the image.

One can think about the poetry of this century in America in these cross-eyed terms: the fluctuations in the distance between these two cats, the actual and the poetic, and the concomitant convictions about what will lessen or collapse that distance. In the debates over form and essence in poetry is mirrored our degree of self-division, and our struggle with it. A compulsive part of our mythology insists our alienation can be overcome in and by means of words.

The struggle to ameliorate such dividedness is also, to my mind, one of the central impulses behind keeping a journal. The separate dimensions of a life lapped together in a notebook produce something extraordinary in its random unshapeliness, something that autobiography with its intentionality perhaps can't even manage. A notebook isn't written; it is kept. It isn't recounted; it is jotted down, accumulated, built up by means of juxtaposition, dispensing with transition, narrative. Unconstrained by form, the pressures of artifice, at times even by the implied eye of a reader, the journal or notebook puts us, at its most striking, in the presence of the created voice of the inner life, rich in tone and feeling.

A journal brings us face to face with its writer in an unmasked guise. Although there is no getting away from guises, the semblance of un-disguise is what we prize. "What dies before me is myself alone:/ What lives? Only a man of straw—/ Yet straw can feed a fire to melt down stone." This is how David Wagoner chooses to begin Roethke's edited notebooks. Stone, the figure for the isolate self; straw, the figure for mercurial poetry. But a notebook need not be brilliant, all fired straw, like Roethke's. It can have the quality of "absolute attention," as Sarton says, quoting Simone Weil on the nature of prayer, or it can appeal to "the amateurs of the unfinished" as Paul Valéry puts it; it can be notational, telegraphic, self-critical.

Perhaps what I am calling un-disguise amounts to the real meaning of subjectivity—world and self deepened by the writer's attention; objects under the writer's gaze all become subjects, things in true relations—and this includes the self. Until then, the self is as much an object as the world is, although harder to see than the world because of its nearness. In the journal's presence we too become subjects; we feel its painful, humanizing touch. This is the intimate aura the jottings and musings of a journal can cast; this may be what, beyond brilliance of idea or observation, we seek them out for.

The notebook excerpts in this anthology for the most part have a narrower frame, in part because they have been necessarily quarried from larger wholes; in part because they were solicited with the purpose of staying close to the craft and subject of poetry. We hoped that a gathering of such prose would give some insight into the working life of poets, their temper and attentiveness and concerns, the blue out of which poetry arises.

—David Weiss

Philip Booth

From the four-hundred-some entries I wrote between June 1960 and November 1965 in the spiral notebook that is a thin Volume IV in the series of such notebooks I began in 1950 as *Fragments,* the following twenty-five entries come from a five-month period exactly thirty years ago.

These entries begin with part of a July-end letter I wrote to an oldest friend the day after I "interrupted" the three-and-a-half years of psychoanalysis which coincided with my final seven semesters of teaching at Wellesley. During July I had taught with John Holmes in his Tufts Poetry Workshop. I went home to Maine for three weeks before moving in September to begin teaching at Syracuse in what would become the Writing Program I was hired to help get started.

That this series of entries untypically includes parts of five letters is, I now think, only one measure of how I was trying to reassure myself, and to write my way *out* of what, for me, was a miserable transition inland. I was, during the summer and fall of 1961, a man hired as a poet who had no poems in him. I had yet to commute back to Boston for intermittent therapy; I had yet to learn from living Upstate the glory of "upland light / fallen through miles of trees."

¶

1961

To D[avid] B[radley], July 29: Such partings are, I suspect, known only to old lovers; it's both like a funeral and being reborn. The wound that woman-surgeon helped me open saved me from something very much like death; I hate her guts for hurting me so, and love her for the healing she has started in my own. Nobody who has not been through it can know, I truly think.... One grows up, maybe, on just such Guadalcanals, and forever knows that no civilian words can get the battle said, or tell what happened when the tracers arc'd in close. One is not cured or much changed, only reinforced where it counts most by having submitted to the battle itself, and having survived. No medals, no merit badges, no report cards, no engraved graduation certificate.

Booth

denly, this first day when the guns are strangely quiet, am like Kilroy: somewhere back in the jungle there is a tree initialled by my knife. I was there. I hope like Christ never to have to return. But I was there; and having been, and come through, gives me, at the very least, more than a fighting chance at not having to go back.

¶

THE COLD COAST
a book of the year's round as
the year turns (with *people*) in Castine.

¶

August: Phil Perkins [Castine's unofficial historian] says that Holman Day was "the poet laureate of Maine, writing about those 'degenerates' in a little town up around Hebron."

¶

August 23: 7 beers, 1 whiskey, 3 gin and tonics, one glass of wine and 1 brandy.

¶

Cal [Lowell], of a breakfast with Jerry [Bruner] and Blanche [Marshall], says that I've "made it" with *The Islanders*. He says that it's "rooted in real earth," that "there's all sorts of solid versification," and that I've staked out Castine as my own (in opposition to the sort of *use* I made of Maine stuff in *Letter*...). The endings, he says, "are different from how I write; they have a kind of dying fall except in poems like 'Propeller.'" He liked the first and last poems ("the right one to end with") especially, also the other "right" ones like "The Owl" and "Propeller" and—surprisingly—"The Anchor." Least of all: "Painter" and "The Round"; but admiration of variousness of prosody, "the WmCWms short-line ones (like 'The Tower') and the long-line ones like 'Jake's Wharf'—one of your best." The tone was what he appeared to like best, "the somewhat hortatory—not exactly this, but this"—flatness and flexibility.

¶

Booth

September: Syracuse-Fayetteville [311 Salt Springs Road]: I'm homesick already and, looking back through these fragments to find old things, it strikes me that the repetitive notes for still unwritten pieces are useful only if to be written *away from* into fictions of which these fragments only define a tone.

¶

Thrumcap

¶

Pip, Ahab's, as Olson rightly sees him: a poem in his own right.

¶

THE TOYS, as in July '55, and the impossibility of freeing the frozen wheel. Black tractor, blue wrecker, green bus: the castiron halves pinned. The woodshed attic.

¶

Not being able to see the North Star.

¶

[Dream]: The big attack on the Castine house. Images of camp (John Moir), V[ermont] A[cademy] ("Tex"), and the fear of losing skis and lack of police protection. The local teddyboys, E[xxxx] C[xxxxx] *et al*, take room after room.

¶

How ironies compound.

¶

Consider: how many poems *La Dolce Vita* makes it unnecessary to write, Fellini's camera having already done that work; yet how many more poems, against the chaos of this very life, the movie demands.

¶

Booth

Quoted in a letter from J[ohn] H[olmes]: "A writer is a man alone in a room with the English language."

❡

    Names of Islands: Ledges:
        Pond   The Brown Cow
        Hog   Ship and Barges
        Butter   Otter Rock
        Sprucehead   Stone Horse
        Horsehead
        Colthead
        Thrumcap
        Ram
        Sheep
        The Virgin's Breasts
        Pumpkin
        Two Bush
        Birch

❡

October: Am I not in too close touch to a lesser reality?

❡

In answer to Charles Olson, October 14: My purpose, as best I know to say it, is only to use right words to define the perhaps meaning of a world I want to love, and to establish some structure of language which —as accurately as possible—reflects my sense of the relationships implicit in that world's superficial disorder. I have to revise even here: I'm trying to talk about poetry as re-seeing, about re-seeing as a way of sensing the world's poetry.

❡

A different language makes, *by definition*, a different kind of statement. Compare the language of Wilbur's "Mind," say, with the language of Denise Levertov's "Matins."

❡

Booth

But the language depends, primarily and irrevocably, on the sense of *time* that underlies & is our major sense of relationship.

¶

I wanted oceans where I lived, a coast to look out somewhere from. Homing here, I came home lost—the Milky Way its own sea and all that, but there are no passages offshore *on my own plane*. That's what haunts me about the Bay: my knowledge there is of headlands, islands, ledges, which are landmarks for how one tacks through them. *Permit Me Voyage* was one great title!

¶

To be well is unlikely; to live well is impossible. To feel well is an absurd possibility, but to think well one can learn.

¶

Today's only the 24th, and I already disagree with part of what I wrote Olson a week ago.

¶

From a letter to Signe Clutz [Wellesley '62]: Don't worry about diving in. Most poetry gets written underwater anyway, at about that level where what's light above filters down into the dark below.

¶

To Ben[son] Snyder [M.D.], December 18: It seems to me that Freud (and all his followers and non-followers) learned deeply from what poets (in the general sense of the word) have written as tragedies: *Oedipus, Hamlet, Lear,* and so on. And that, as all analysts—from Freud's concern with Irma's Injection to The Botanical Monograph, etc.— have been terrifyingly involved in potential tragedy, they tend to write about analysis with a necessarily defensive dispassion which Sophocles or Shakespeare neither needed nor wanted. Tragedy deals dramatically in fatal *acts*. But analysis, a drama without action, is a *comedy*. Did I not weep, hate, love, get gut-struck, and shake until I was

13

Booth

cold? I did. Did I not imagine that I had caused my mother's death by violating a prime taboo, and that I could or would kill my father to earn my way free of such violation? I did. But somehow, in retrospect, it seems to me that I continually could see myself *pretending* to those acts of tragic consequence. As Dr. F. continually reinforced what I suppose was my ego, she kept such sight in my mind. But was it not fundamentally *comic* that I imagined that I was *unique* in imagining such tragic possibilities? The tragic hero, *acting* on his sense of uniqueness, *acts* to create tragedy (tragedy because he has partial self-knowledge). But to realize that one is not unique (in wanting, masochistically, as a martyr, to act on such impulse) is to see one's self as fool protagonist in a comedy of errors. Analysis, in truth, is the world's greatest and most lonely comedy; analysts (and ex-analysands who, still identifying, wish they were analysts) will write well about analysis only when they learn to laugh with (not at) themselves and their patients. What madness (literally) it is to believe that one is *uniquely* committed to murder and incest. But what a saving grace it is, in whatever painful comedy, to realize that so to feel capable of acting (without *having* to act) is to join the human race. Do we lose our unique individuality in so admitting we are human? Hardly. We begin, I begin to find, to give up wasting *this* sense of uniqueness in order to be unique in the meaningfully mature ways of which we are humanly capable.

¶

From a letter to J[ames] W[right], December 27 [which refers to "First Draft," a poem in *The Islanders*]: If a few of us don't survive, none of us will. We are bound, in spite of the fools we are, by the words we risk being true to. "The late fog, lifting" is a sentence, and it sentences us to be true to the pure fact we can learn to act on. Myths, as they were true for the one man who wrote them, become the factual basis of how we learn to live. Fiction they may be, but they state a truth truer than so-called non-fiction will ever know. The world is a poem, as my poem to you tried to get said, and we can only write it by cutting away the prose as a sculptor chips at stone to discover the figure the grain of the stone contains. I think we marry that figure, and I think, if we will, we write ourselves into the truth we've pared away falsehood to find.

Sharon Bryan

Jean Baudrillard: Photography is not a mirror but a hall of mirrors (perfect image for language).

¶

Finding a way to love things without despairing because they'll come to an end—and we will.

¶

Creeley essays: nostalgia (for Black Mtn). How are avant-garde and nostalgia related—rather than being opposites? Their emphasis on the ephemeral?

¶

Vivid images tempt us to believe we can see around language, contact the world on our own, without the help of a medium.

¶

Radio—writing is like tuning into a station, daily life is the static—or at least daily life we don't like.

¶

When people compare their memories of the same event, the details don't always mesh—like railroad tracks laid from two directions.

¶

Painting is inherently metaphysical, philosophical. Is that true of writing, literature? Yes, but it's easier to forget, since the medium of literature is also used in daily life.

¶

"Cerebral"—why should this be a bad thing for poems to be? And what can it mean? Maybe it means knowing more things from outside the poem than inside the poem; the intellect not sufficiently balanced by the emotions. But surely one reinforces the other, or can. E.g., Bach.

¶

Bryan

Leaf-covered car: like driving a float in a fall parade.

⁋

Miracle: something unlikely (recovery)—but always good. Why doesn't *bad* luck count as a miracle, when it's as rare an event?

⁋

Restaurants. The oddity of paying to eat out with other people—when did it begin?

⁋

Reading Whitman, after watching two wars: Ken Burns' Civil War and George Bush's Persian Gulf War:

> For my enemy is dead, a man as divine as myself is dead,
> I look where he lies white-faced and still in the coffin—I draw near,
> Bend down and touch lightly with my lips the white face in the coffin.

⁋

Rimbaud: "… wasn't the flesh a fruit hanging in the orchard? … wasn't the body a treasure to spend?"

⁋

The Enemy: from now on POW will refer only to our people captured by the enemy. EPW means "enemy prisoners of war," the ones we hold.

⁋

Southern spring—too quick and easy, like bad sex.

⁋

> Oriole
> An angel with a cloak
> thrown over its shoulders,
> or the devil in a flashy tie.

⁋

> She's just singing a little song
> about everything gone wrong,
> and his saxophone says, You're right,
> I'm leaving you alone tonight.

¶

General to soldiers: You've been to places whose names you can't even pronounce.

¶

Milosz: If a problem is stated in the wrong terms, it can't be solved.

He assumed movie details to be inventions, rather than actual details of life lived elsewhere. (That's how, growing up in a desert, I thought of forests large enough to get lost in.)

One is safe and invisible in the forest.

¶

Poetry as simply the turnings (of phrase) from one line to the next, the shifting weight, point of view, pivots. The very definition of verse.

¶

Little things that change (or set) the key, tone, of a day, the way dreams do. An unexpected parade, for example.

¶

Atrocities: real test of the imagination re reality. The common wisdom: your imagination is worse than any actualities—but that's not true. Someone imagined more horrible things *and* then carried them out. So in a way, it comes back to the imagination, what we do with it.

¶

Women of Plums (poems based on slave journals):

griot: storyteller; he and the stolen people were lost to each other.

Bryan

I'm dead.
I know it 'cause I'm happy.

Evil be pretty sometimes, don't it?

¶

Abstract art (Pollock) is as close as painting can get to making us listen instead of look.

¶

The difference between hearing and seeing atrocities.

¶

Music may move through time, but it opens space.

¶

Sight is completely bound to the present. Not just: *I see*, but *I am seeing*—and even then we're turning it into a story, past tense.

¶

Most of language is about what we've overheard, not what we know firsthand.

¶

Talleyrand: speech is "a faculty given to man to conceal his thoughts."

¶

The relationship between present tense and the rest of our lives—it's a kind of continuo or ground bass, the ground against which we tell stories, rather than the figure—except (maybe) when something is so vivid it slows time and becomes the foreground.

¶

Fraser (on time): language is one of the ways we deal with the anxiety produced by our realization that we'll die.

¶

Everything not in present tense is a work of the imagination.

※

Why do we pull a sheet over the faces of the dead? Why do we cover our eyes instead of just closing them when we're afraid?

※

Tanglewood: The ritual of it. Why is music the most spiritual art? What an odd thing, all of us gathered around sounds in the air. The Eroica. Acoustical ceiling, like bats flying out of a cave. The difference between seeing a concert and listening to one.

※

Typo in newspaper story on fatal fire: "He fell three stories from his death."

※

Fitzgerald: "Show me a hero and I'll write you a tragedy." Used about Pete Rose.

※

Plath couldn't invent. Believed vision is fact, not one more illusion. So she couldn't escape things, could only embellish them.

※

Difference between Dickinson and Plath: ED began with the assumption that the "real world" is a construction, an illusion. Plath took things, the world of appearances, for something objective, hard fact, something that she couldn't get around.

※

Shakespeare, "The Rape of Lucrece": "To see sad sights moves more than to hear them told/ For then the eye interprets the ear."

I don't agree—the mind's eye is more powerful.

※

Bryan

Mother to child in a grocery store, after her son had dropped his money and a woman had pointed it out to him: "You have to learn to be more careful. If a black person had found that, he probably wouldn't have given it back."

¶

Mother of murder victim: "I just really thought he would kill her, he loved her so."

¶

Writing and the Body, Gabriel Josipovici: Writing and speaking are at the crossroads of mental and physical, cultural and natural.

¶

After reading Stella:

For the artist (and for others?), our absence and our presence are identical—the presence of the work implies both the making hand and the shape that puts the reader or spectator in the artist's shoes: the artist is what's missing from the picture, the poem.

Different approaches are required for works that seem to face us, be in dialogue with us, and those that look out onto the world, so we must take their viewpoint.

¶

Barfield: First we killed off nature as it had been, then we personified it.

¶

What's the difference between knowing that a friend is absent but alive and knowing that the friend is dead?

¶

On not having children: In the Chicago Aquarium, on Family Day, it suddenly seems a strange thing to do, to create more people—not when it's done out of love, pleasure, etc.—but that it so often seems to be thoughtless, a failure of imagination—why create more people when there are already so many to get to know? Seems like a lot to do with fear, insecurity, a need to have power over people we're going to be close to, by growing them ourselves. Incredible relief at not having a life that revolves around children.

❡

Poverty: Elvis—in some ways the problem was poverty of the imagination, what to do with all that money. How poverty cramps your dreams—you either don't imagine anything that costs money, or you imagine some tacky, expensive twin of the poor life: a gold-plated piano. You imagine only more layers on the familiar, not something new. Live in a fantasy world rather than an imaginative one. Difference between fantasy and imagination: fantasy replaces reality, becomes a way *not* to act. Imagination is active, fantasy is passive.

❡

Poverty: anger, beginning with the self, but turned outward. Gluttony, obesity—partly malnutrition, bad religion (what does that mean? Again, without imagination, literal-minded; deferred rewards).

Poverty: fear—of almost everything, including change.

❡

Prosperity: are more rich people unhappy, or do they just have more visible, more spectacular unhappiness? The pluses and minuses of leisure time. Mobility. Consumers of art, though producers of art are poor, usually. The rich have access—to people, places, good tables in restaurants, medical care, views, resources, education. Power. Sense of entitlement, ownership.

❡

Essay on ambition: Distinguish ambition from pretension. Bishop's modesty (see Kalstone)—though she studied Latin and Greek, had been accepted at Cornell Medical School, knew how to fish, knew art

Bryan

and music, traveled. The deceptively simple surfaces, complex depths. Many contemporary poems that pass for "ambitious" are all unnecessarily complicated surface, little depth.

Douglas Crase

1987

January 1: At precisely midnight when the firecrackers began to go off I looked out the bedroom window toward Times Square and, better than fireworks, saw Ursa Major standing on her tail directly over the Elliott-Chelsea Houses. The year starts in the cool, unstartled stars—as we are in fact in Ursa Major as it disperses, opening out to Deneb or beyond.

¶

January 5: Right-to-life is a metaphor adopted by the deathliest people. Does Nature believe you have a right to life? The HIV virus does not think so, nor do the businessmen manufacturing bombs. The nation, likewise, is a metaphor for something that has long since ceased to exist in terms of active power, or virtue. It is a market, yes, to multinational corporations, but it is not their nation. It is a source of subsidy for the defense industry, but it is not what they defend. It is not there.

¶

January 17: I took Frank to the airport this morning & stopped off at Achkinkesacking on the way home: a hawk at the landfill, the pond frozen over, song sparrows in the stiff dead weeds along the causeway—and in the flats the most beautiful male shoveler, there in that once desolation. Looking flat to the sun, his head is black; looking out of the sun, green; & half into the sun, purple. The eye always yellow—& that chestnut flank. He seemed to follow me. Colder than shit, & the landfill very busy with dumpsters.

One difference between you and the modernists, you and the critical wisdom, is gratitude. Those brief moments, the intimations of a world in ecstasy—for them you are grateful and you hold on to them. You are not going to deny them because they don't happen every day. But the others, the "realists" who still like to make fun of the sixties, say, are as little boys who, having been disappointed once, aren't going to let you catch them being disappointed ever again. They deny even their first experience of ecstasy its reality. Rather than being grateful for having

Crase

seen, they curse sight because they can't have it whenever they want it, all the time. Who is being naive?

❡

January 18: Snow all morning, and wonderful. From Weehawken you could not see across the river. I went looking for our hawk, because it irritated me all night I wasn't sure which one he was. No surprise, he was in the same tree. My stopping brought a second observer in a van. Hard to tell at first: but a third car scared him off to a different tree, and there in the January light, the thick snow light, was the rufous tail. I thought if I stayed watching him long enough somehow Frank could see him too.

❡

January 19: One thing you can't do is characterize, much less condemn, whole generations. When Vietnam came along, they called a whole generation selfish, spoiled, because it would hold them and their country to their revolutionary word. *Our* leaders (as if leaders were wanted) being assassinated & discredited has left *them* in control even to this day: and what have they done with that control? They have presided over the dismantling of liberty, industry, the dollar, foreign trade, the phone service, railroads; they have pillaged, destroyed & vandalized—they the most aggressively selfish and spoiled generation ever set loose on this country—& have left to us and to our children a diminished estate & fateful downward mobility: the first generation since the Revolution to face such inescapable diminishment. The Second World War may have been a war America could not choose to ignore, but it has been an unmitigated disaster for all that was once called American: for the land, for American virtue, for democracy, for the future, for American antimilitarism, for what was once called American independence. What we have left is an internationalist superstructure of economic and cultural privilege that can now seek only to pacify or suppress the Liverpools, Manchesters & Boltons it has left behind all over the United States, the Scotlands & Irelands & Haitis it has left behind on lands where Emerson & Louis Sullivan imagined lions of the West instead, where Whitman could imagine a place (in Ohio!) where the perfect personalities without noise meet. Can you say poetry is not to be read against this radical disappointment?

¶

January 31: More taxis spotted: Gist Cab, Godspeed Taxi, Random Cab, Puddle Taxi, & the driver—honest—was taking a piss.

¶

February 3: I locate those of our generational persuasion from birthdate 1939, when the first volunteers left for the Canadian RAF, to 1946, when the draftees came home. Hence: Frank Bidart, Pinsky, McMichael & Hass, Ann Lauterbach, Susan Howe & Marjorie Welish, John Koethe, Paul Hoover & Vicki Hearne.

¶

February 6: With Marjorie I was too happy to agree: it is not America as a trope for renewal and resistance that I love and want to protect. What I want to protect is America herself, the very body of her, her arms, legs, swell & dip—goldenrod hills of her. It is this body that has been exploited and ravaged and vandalized by those who think of her only as an abstraction. Not the trope, but the real sunswept tilt of her—never to be ignored, to be sidelined, to be exterminated again.

¶

February 10: I am a populist, though we're all so awful, because I know one of us is just like me.

¶

February 27: My answer to Marjorie is: On Treason Hill. Benedict Arnold thought America was a trope, too.

¶

Crase

March 2: People! and I am as dislocated as an animal that has been picked up out of its path &, when replaced, must cower & turn around five times to find out where it was.

¶

April 5: It is not enough to love something. Love doesn't preserve—doesn't preserve, protect, or defend.

¶

April 7: Donald Davie reviews W. C. Williams the way Fenton did Ashbery, as though poetry were a game to be played in a zero-sum society, in which the poet sees a certain role or position open up & shrewdly fills it. One would like to hear what Williams would say about the Englishness of that.

¶

April 19: Poetry is the moment we are free. It does not devalue or inauthenticate poetry if in other moments we are not free. In the moment you are a transparent eyeball you experience true freedom, functionally true while it is happening. If the freedom is not made universal, this is no fault of the poem but a condition of fate: we will die, there is no permanent freedom ever. But to say that freedom in poetry is no good because we can't always be free is like saying sex is no good because we can't always be doing it. If you cannot have sex, have as much as you can. If you cannot be free, be as free as you can.

¶

April 24: They say hyperbole is when the language strains against the realities that constrain us: every time I, for instance, return my argument to "America."

¶

May 20: There are professors who believe the Royalists to form a continuous part of our tradition—to *be* our tradition—which is not only ahistorical but a kind of treason. The first Emerson, Emerson's great-

great-great-great-grandfather Thomas, was in Ipswich in 1638, so soon (five years) after the publication in England of George Herbert's poems that, gee, maybe he didn't have time to pick up a copy before he left.

❡

May 28: This morning in Clement Moore Park in the first Gleditsia: a yellow warbler, singing madly, and a northern parula, driven off by the yellow. Then the parula alone in the second Gleditsia, now singing himself.

❡

May 29: Why not an *evolutional* imperative? So act, and so write, that the rule by which you operate could be adopted universally without obstructing the process of evolution. Thus jetties, which obstruct the evolution of a beach, violate the evolutional imperative. Thus nuclear explosions on earth, which return time and matter to a more primitive state, violate the evolutional imperative. Thus prejudice, which obstructs the progress of a democracy of options, of the evolutional increase in mobility evidenced by living things. Drunkenness, which obstructs the advance of thought into lonely places so as to make them less lonely. In a way, psychoanalysis—at least too transfixedly pursued—violates the evolutional imperative. Oppressions of all kinds violate it. Rhyme and antique meter and sestinas and sonnets violate it. The universe expands, and whatever seeks to stop the expansion violates this imperative. Thus specism, which denies the planet as a field of action to any but one species, violates the evolutional imperative—likewise all the concomitants of specism, the specist prejudice against abortion, birth control, homosexuality, and decent self-chosen death.

❡

May 30: The reason it takes so long is: I reason by syllables.

❡

Crase

June 1: You wouldn't ask an English lawyer to try a case in American law because he knows English law, yet we ask the English critic to judge American poetry because he knows…English.

¶

June 8: The task is to preserve American prophecy from the long reach of European eschatologies. There is no somewhere from which our conduct will be approved, no elsewhere that is superior to this *here*. There can be no appeal, no forgiveness from Europe or extraterrestrial beings or even the Universe. On Earth we are functionally alone, just as the Americans were. This is why their experience still avails.

¶

June 9: The John Winthrop kind of liberty has been exhumed by the new neos, and the flacks and sourpusses have begun bawling about the need to surrender personal liberty in service to the community. Even the Supreme Court's perfidious Hardwick decision may, in the back of the judges' putative brains, seem to them to express such deference. But the experience of the American wilderness has shown that civil insistence is not enough. The evolutional purpose of community is to set free the individual, otherwise everywhere trapped in Nature and in nature's true totalitarian commune, death.

¶

June 22: Really, what alternative is there to having a subject?

¶

June 26: At lunch at the Sazerac House on Wednesday, I: "No one will dare to say the word 'impeach' until some institution calls for it." Marjorie: "Or some logo."

Guy Davenport

August 30, 1989–January 8, 1991

The wasp carries his wife from aster to pear.

❡

A Plymouth Brethren chapel, or hall as they say, on the Faeroes. William Sloan, Scots missionary of the Plymouth Brethren, converted the Faeroes in 1865. The Danes call them *Baptistar*, or the *sekt*. They are abstemious. "Beer," they say, "is another man".

❡

A March laundry line of oystercatchers. Drifting acres of glare on the sea, clouds grazing the chimneys. Oystercatchers like wash lines in March.

❡

Randolph Bourne's idea that critical discernment is in knowing why we like what we like is intelligent and wise. He was disturbed that education in art is geared to an imposed canon. Our problem now is that nobody knows anything to begin with. A love of knowledge is gone, and with it curiosity and a critical eye. We have theory instead of perception, contentiousness instead of discussion, dogma instead of inquiry.

❡

Jaako Hintikka, philosopher and critic of Wittgenstein. In private life a reindeer.

❡

"Not ashamed to sin but ashamed to repent" (Defoe). A motto for Kentucky.

❡

Davenport

Neither Kafka nor Donald Barthelme could have written an autobiography.

¶

Crusoe was on his island for the 35 years before the landing of William III at Torbay (which he mentions as the place of a shipwreck). Defoe was among William's soldiers. Friday was the empire.

¶

A life is a secret.

¶

Freudian analysis turned out to be insensitive to the very values which give art its identity, as deconstruction is a hostile cross-examination of a helpless witness.

¶

An American reading Lévi-Strauss is in the peculiar position of a person without a civilization reading a person from a highly civilized country writing about culture. In some sense we do not know what he means. "Hell is other people." But for the American the Other does not exist. We are solipsists. We are not individuals, as the individual does not exist except in a culture. No culture, no individual (who can only be an example of a culture). So we must read Lévi-Strauss as people he's writing about rather than for.

¶

The USA and the USSR have exhausted their inherited European culture.

¶

In our century the great event has been the destruction of the city, and therefore of public life, by the automobile. Next, the obliteration of the family by television. Thirdly, the negation of the university by its transformation into a social club for nonstudents. Fourthly, the abandonment of surveillance by the police, who act only upon request and arrive long after their presence could be of any use. All of this can be blamed on the stupidity, moral indifference, and ignorance of politicians and public alike.

※

There's a Dutch philosopher in Groeningen who charges $40 an hour for Wittgensteinian solutions to problems. "They know the answers. It's their questions they aren't aware of."

※

Jane Kramer says that the French prefer a common etiquette to a common ground. We all do, I think. It's Lévi-Strauss's table manners as a technique of culture. Boring and impossible people are primarily violators of etiquette, imposing a different sense of space, time, periodicity.

※

High-minded principles and intolerance are twins. The word *liberal* has over the past fifty years come to mean *illiberal*. Not only illiberal: puritanical, narrow-minded, mean.

※

Avoid the suave flow of prose that's the trademark of the glib writer. An easy and smooth style is all very well, but it takes no chances and has no seductive wrinkles, no pauses for thought.

※

It was Bourdelle who advised Rodin to clothe his "Balzac."

※

The emptier a room the smaller it seems. This is true of minds as well.

※

PHYTOLITH. *Nardus stricta* contains phytoliths which could not be mistaken for those from any other of the grasses. Microscopic bits of crystal from the soil appearing in plants.

※

A sixty is a flower pot $3\frac{1}{2}''$ in diameter, so called from sixty of them being thrown from the one batch of clay.

※

"Hibiscus!" said the lion. "Isaiah!" the owl replied. The moon was white, was round, was rising. Bartók, the cicadas.

※

The way into Rimbaud is through his meadows.

※

Michel was, he supposed, happy. He was not certain what happy was, but his happiness had been noticed and specified. Once, when he was smaller, his class had gone to the museum to see Eskimo things, and he had, while their teacher was showing them a kayak, taken off his shoes and socks to count his toes. Suzanne said, "O mère de…look at Michel!" Teacher had said, placidly, "Michel is happy."

※

Isak Dinesen's meadows at Rungsted. Beyond an apple orchard. Her grave is under a great beech.

※

Forty finches in the thistles. In the high summer of time.

The road, always the road, olive and fig on hills, fields yellow with wheat.

Their footsteps made the silence creak. Thomas, the twin, talking.

—Rabbi, this tearing off of the foreskin, is it right?

Yeshua's answers were always quick, as if he knew what you were going to say.

—If the Everlasting had wanted us to have no foreskin, we would be born without one. Nothing should be shorn that does not grow back.

Thomas looking around Yeshua's hat to study his eyes in the brim's shadow.

Yeshua's smiling irony.

—If our bodies are designed by the Everlasting for our souls, what a wonder!

Yeshua talking, talking with the sweet patience of the fellowship, to Thomas and Simon and John, and to someone else also. They had remarked on this among themselves, that their company sometimes included an unseen other.

—But if our souls are created for the body's sake, that would be the wonder of wonders. The Egyptians elongate the infant's skull while it is still soft, and there are those beyond our sea who bind their women's feet and picture their skins all over with needles and ink, and file their teeth. Only the subtle Greeks, whose Herakleitos could parse the grammar of creation and whose Pythagoras discovered the harmony of numbers, leave the healthy body intact.

A stonechat dipped and sailed sideways. Yeshua put out his hand, and the stonechat came and sat on it, head cocked.

Yeshua speaking to the stonechat, in its Latin.

—Is the flesh then good? Thomas asked.

—Is there, Yeshua asked, perhaps of the stonechat, perhaps of Thomas, Simon, and John, any other way of being? The Everlasting's work is all one creation. Are we to say of the only creation there is that it is nasty?

¶

Horses buck, cocks crow. Cat dogs one's steps. Dog badgers. A subset of animal words. To squirrel away things, to cow one's enemy, to horse around, to ferret out, to weasel, to parrot, to canary, to ape.

¶

> Many russet-clad children
> Lurking in these broad meadows
> With the bittern and the woodcock
> Concealed by brake and hardhack.

¶

Samuel Palmer. Moss sopped in gold clotted on the thatch of a roof. Mr. Christian trudging by.

¶

"When angry, paint bamboo."—Wang Mien (1335–1415)

¶

The white frost that made the fire feel so good, and the quilt so comfortable, had also reddened the maples and mellowed the persimmons. Cloth shoes stink by the fire. Foxes bark in the deep of the wind.

¶

Opossum:persimmon::moth:mulberry. Christmas Island (South Pacific): imperial pigeon, noddy, glossy swiftlet, reef heron.

¶

To see a clock as a clock, Wittgenstein said, is the same as seeing Orion striding in the stars.

¶

Queneau on Fourier as a mathematician, making Marx more of a Fouriériste than an Hegelian.

¶

> No force however great
> Can stretch a thread however fine
> Into a horizontal line
> That is absolutely straight.

(A prose sentence in a textbook, by sheer accident a Tennysonian stanza. There's a Yeatsian sonnet so disguised in *The Counterfeiters* of Hugh Kenner.)

¶

Hemingway's prose is like an animal talking. But what animal?

Rita Dove

1980

Strike a stone
to see if it's thinking of water.

❡

Ivory Gate

Tom sleepwalking—when are you going to take me fishing?

I love you and you (don't) love me
It is not exactly like
drinking the sea.

Here we go round the
coconut tree
It is not exactly like
drinking the sea.

❡

The Projects.

Washing lines of the poor—the banners.

>shut you up & out.
>brick, housing art.

❡

Arson: houses mysteriously bursting into flame.

>language is identity.

It was hotter: they wanted it hotter.

❡

I was so handsome women cried,
I got shot but never died.
>—Cher, "A Cowboy's Work Is Never Done"

❡

Dove

The buffalo faces the storm from the west;
therefore its hair is thicker in front,
and he gets out of the storm quicker.

¶

We drove through olive
    fields quartz and dust,
their petticoats hiked up
above our heads; small reward
for the assiduous, small gain
for aesthetics, this dive
    thru butterflies
& dust.

¶

Purse as womb.

¶

A porcelain cup overturned on a plate: an iridescent igloo.

¶

1987–89

"When you begin to write, you're in love with the language, with the act of creation, with yourself partly; but as you go on, the writing—if you follow it—will take you places you never intended to go and show you things you would never otherwise have seen. I began as a profoundly apolitical writer, but then I began to do what all novelists and some poets do: I began to describe the world around me."
                      —Margaret Atwood, in an interview
                         with *Ms.* magazine, January, 1987.

¶

Dove

Jerusalem as interpreted by Zali: 12/4/87

First to the graves from 8 B.C., behind the Scottish Hospice. Incredibly chaotic traffic. Z. explains that the valley between us and the Old City was called *Gehenna*, or Hell, and was the place where human sacrifices were made. The graves, vaults carved from rock, are on a slope called Kebet (?), or the Shoulder of Hell. There are light bulb-shaped hollows for the heads, and a vault situated between an L-shaped cadaver cache that had been filled with treasures—vases, urns, oil lamps, etc.

Here you can see the absence of bodies more vividly than the bodies themselves must have been. The entire area is littered with shit—literally curlicues of shit, garbage, Pepsi ringtops, plastic bags in all colors. And then one looks straight up into the blond foundations of the hospice, its stalwart honey-colored cross on top.

Zali tells us about his personal relationship to the Burnt House, discovered in the Old City in the Jewish Quarter, directly across from the Wailing Wall. Many many meters below today's surface, a ruin of a house was found—carbon-dating sets its destruction at 70 A.D., the same year that the Romans destroyed the Temple. Found were the implements of daily life, plus an arm bone of a man, plus a sword that, judging from its position, was thrust into the body belonging to the arm. And a nameplate was found, carved into stone with the name of a priestly family mentioned in the chronicles of Josephus Flavius.

Zali says he learned about the Burnt House upon his return from Berkeley, and he feels as if he is fated, that he carries the Burnt House inside him, that his communion with 70 A.D. and Josephus Flavius has been burnt into him.

This is the direct time axis that only Jerusalem has—eons piled on top of eons, so many eons that it is impossible to fence them off and charge admission. Hence these sights are the true discoveries, *real* artifacts at dirt level, clear and clean as the shapes of bodies outlined in the rubble and donkey droppings.

Dove

(The idea of the Burnt House, a plunge into History, a telescoping of time on the one hand and the smoldering grief that inures on the other—this is contained in the appellation:
The Burnt House—
a heartbreak.

The Burnt House: a rebellion of a neighborhood—
Firetraps on fire, determined to turn into their names.)

Then we go to the newly built promenade in Talpiot with its magnificent view of Jerusalem, where one understands the phrase *Jerusalem, mountains around her*—for the Old City (which is the only Jerusalem) is surrounded, set off by hills, like a jewel that draws all sight to it: it shines. Here, Z says, you can see what makes Jerusalem different, for it is a city that draws its inhabitants inward—the very setting is a centripetal force drawing all thought, all contemplation, inward. A city of introspection ... whereas Tel Aviv looks outward, toward the sea. Z tells us of the time he flew over Mt. Scopus in a plane while on reserve duty. As a professor, he had always simply driven up the hill, parked and gone into the university; the hill was part of the city, of his daily life. From the air, however, he could see that Mount Scopus (named so because it was the vantage point citizens—including Josephus Flavius—climbed up to in order to look down upon the Temple, which in those days had been covered in gold) was the last ridge before desert, desert, desert. From the air he realized that Jerusalem was *in* the desert, that it *was* a desert town. And the original Israelites who had moved in and built the first temple, were a desert culture—they didn't like nature with its trees and bushes, they didn't like sex or good food—they liked meat without the sauce.

So Z calls forth another axis in Israel—the cultural axis, Tel Aviv to Jerusalem, a mere 70 kilometers but really a swing from Mediterranean to desert.

Another axis is the nature axis, north to south, from vegetation to barrenness. And so Jerusalem (my interpretation) is the original Axis

Dove

Mundi, the earth rotating on a spit like a *Baumkuchen* that grows crust after crust.

¶

Jean Follain: often had nightmares that he could have been born two years later and would not have remembered the time before the first World War ... when the archetypes were clear.

    a) The soldiers would meet people who had experienced this great calm, and for whom the world made no sense anymore.

    b) The soldiers, though, come from a world without a backyard (back porch); they know a world that is senseless.

Don't forget all the plays of colloquial language.

Check book for direct quotes from soldiers.

You must learn French.

—The March to the Rhine
—Lt. James Europe's Jazz Band

Our terrible century (W.S. Merwin)

The Romans were a race of travellers/tourists

¶

Ars Poetica—"Build a cell in your mind, from which you can never escape."
                      —Catherine of Siena

¶

Overheard on stewardesses' P.A. system, in between flights—Phoenix-Dallas-LaGuardia:

    Pilot: Ladies, we're ready to board now, we'll need two pluckers up front. (Pause) Ladies *and* gentlemen ...

    Chief Stewardess: It's show time.

¶

Dove

> Ample make this bed
> Make this bed in awe
> In it wait till Judgement break
> Excellent and fair
>
> Be its mattress straight
> Be its pillow round
> Let no sunrise yellow noise
> Interrupt this ground
> —Emily Dickinson

(Written out by Bruce Weigl during a heated discussion at the April 1988 AWP board meeting)

❡

"Christianity is, from its inception (Paul), the romantic religion. The cult of love in the West is an aspect of the cult of suffering—suffering as the supreme token of seriousness (the paradigm of the Cross)."
—Susan Sontag
The Artist as Exemplary Sufferer

"The writer is the man who discovers the use of suffering in the economy of art—as the saints discovered the utility and necessity of suffering in the economy of salvation."
—Susan Sontag, *ibid*.

❡

Title for a section (poetry)—"The low grounds of sorrow" from G.W. Carver, referring to the poor farmland given to the poor blacks.

❡

14th c.—Venetians cut down Yugoslavian forest for their fleets—which destroyed the land (topsoil blown away) and changed the climate.

Dove

Ozone layer

Now you see it
Now you don't

The glass is tipped
The plug pulled

Afghani—knitting is too intricate, too microscopic and small town/world.

Terraces of the Doge—from far they look like quiltwork, but they, too, are more like knitting, weaving the rocks without mortar into a wall to stand 400 years.

And the wake of the motorboat
braiding, braiding
And the world tipped upside
down, the plug pulled,
draining out its vital fluid
         (ozone)

¶

Afghani Nomad Coat

A beastiary
A breviary

¶

Jet lag, and the home space
stapled onto the bow of the world;
each desert papery bloom a fluttery paste-up,
purple trumpets of sage,
tiny mustard pockets of sage purses

¶

As my daughter said on the way to K-Mart: "Everyone was inside someone else once."

¶

Dove

[Thomas Hardy] told a friend that he wanted to avoid "the jeweled life"; his awkwardness, often an ostentation, laboriousness, was both natural and cultivated. He is the first of the poets, so numerous now, who are suspicious of writing well.

… he said that "Art is a disproportioning of realities, to show more clearly the features that matter in those realities."

Stephen Dunn

One perception must immediately lead to another perception, as Olson said, is another way of saying that a poem should be interesting *all* the way through.

❡

When people praise a poem that I can't understand I always think they're lying.

❡

The problem with most nature poetry is that it doesn't sufficiently acknowledge Nature's ugliness and perversity. It is as falsifying as most poems about happy marriages.

❡

Poems about happy marriages need to be mysterious. A successful happy marriage poem, like a happy marriage itself, is a triumph over the unlikely. You must write it with the inventive care with which you would write science fiction.

❡

Mystifications protect power. Mysteries protect the sacred.
—John Berger

❡

Every male has a stake in feminism. Obviously it is not a good situation for anybody when one sex has earned the greater right to complain. And don't happy women tend to be generous? Self-interest, if not basic decency, should convince men that a fair-minded feminism is also their liberation. All of us, finally, free enough to be scoundrels.

❡

The poets who defy making sense and do it deliberately and often brilliantly (as Ashbery can) *are* making a kind of sense, and may be extending the range of what poetry can do, though they rarely give me pleasure.

❡

Authenticity in literature does not come from a writer's personal honesty ... Authenticity comes from a single faithfulness: that to the ambiguity of experience ... If a writer is not driven by a desire for the most demanding verbal precision, the true ambiguity of events escapes him.
—John Berger

❧

When I've had an interesting or haunting dream, I know I'd better not try to write about it until it has begun to bore me a little.

❧

A perfectly modulated sentence, one that discloses its information at just the right pace, is a victory over what is crude and easy and careless about the way we think and feel. A paragraph of such sentences has the sufficiency of a well-made sculpture. About its content, we're likely to say "That's true." What we mean is how persuasively the meaning is being displayed and held.

❧

After the superb dance concert (Momix) the other night, I felt so elated and enlarged that I knew what I should expect of poetry readings.

❧

"Sometimes," said Whitey Ford, the great Yankee curveballer, "you need to put one right down the middle." He was speaking of surprises. I've always thought that poets, especially abstruse poets, could profit by his remark.

❧

I dream of an art so transparent that you can look through and see the world.
—Stanley Kunitz

❧

Finally, what I want from poetry is akin to what Flaubert wanted from novels. He thought they should make us dream. I want a poem, through its precisions and accuracies, to make me remember what I know, or what I might have known if I hadn't been constrained by convention or habit.

❡

In a sense, my father was a Willy Loman. He was my introduction to the pathetic and to sadness and heroism. I don't know how I escaped Biff's escapism, his self-destructiveness. But I did. Perhaps it was because when things went bad I still had the esteem of the schoolyard. For a long important while I didn't have to think, except as an athlete does. I just played ball. Sweet moves and the ball in the hole. The pure poetry that satisfies when you're young.

❡

My maternal grandfather's name was Montefiore Fleischman. I grew up in his house, a Dunn. He was a story-teller, a lover of women, perhaps a great man. In his sixties, he read a novel and drank a bottle of gin every night. Arthritic, it was how he achieved sleep.

❡

The erotics of memory.
—Joyce Carol Oates

❡

He remembered a great deal, but the memory was uninteresting, tedious, and he was even a little annoyed at its tenacity.
—Anita Brookner

❡

The invented person, borrowed from the real—abstracted, isolated—is the person we finally know, or feel we know. I make myself up from everything I am, or could be. For many years I was more desire than fact. When I stop becoming, that's when I worry.

❡

Too many poets are insufficiently interested in story. Their poems could be improved if they gave in more to the strictures of fiction: the establishment of a clear dramatic situation, and a greater awareness that first-person narrators are also characters and must be treated as such by their authors. The true lyric poet, of course, is exempt from this. But many poets wrongly think they are lyric poets.

¶

I hate good taste. Those who say they have it exhibit its opposite.

¶

As Kafka put it, there is an infinite amount of hope, but not for us. This statement really contains Kafka's hope; it is the source of his radiant serenity.
—Walter Benjamin

¶

The world, finally, tries to rob us in lots of ways. I like poems to do a bit of taking back for us.
—Terry Blackhawk

¶

Fall seven times, stand up eight.
—Japanese Proverb

¶

Edward Hopper said that "Painting will have to deal more fully and less obliquely with life and nature's phenomena before it can again become great." So will poetry. Yet that won't be enough. It will require compositional skills and angles of vision equal to Hopper's.

¶

The tyranny of the actual begins.
— Philip Roth

¶

Dunn

Lovers are unreliable witnesses, which is why reliability is not always to be desired.

¶

Mickey Rivers, a former Yankee centerfielder, when asked if he was worried about being traded, said something I try to remember to live by when things are going bad. "Ain't no sense in worrying about things you got control over, 'cause if you got control over them, ain't no sense worrying. And there ain't no sense worrying about things you got no control over, 'cause if you got no control over them, ain't no sense worrying."

¶

Lewis Hyde's book *The Gift* made me, for a while, more generous. For about two weeks, I wanted to give everything away. Barry Lopez's book *Arctic Dreams*, equally moral and powerful, made me want to write graceful yet heavily freighted sentences. I value both books, but I'll return more often to *Arctic Dreams*.

¶

I don't think I'd complain if I were overrated.

¶

I believe everything you tell me, but I know that it will all turn out differently.   —Henry Miller

¶

I don't trust people until I know what they love. If they cannot admit to what they love, or in fact love nothing, I cannot take even their smartest criticisms seriously.

¶

Can I change myself with some discoloration, that unclearness I despise in the work of other men? And what should I avoid? Anything contrived. Anything less than vital.

— John Cheever

¶

Summertime, the children older now, 17 & 20, their noise more quiet than in the past, but noise nonetheless. I realize how comforting those sounds are, the sounds that for years I complained about and worked to. I should admit it, silence has given me more trouble than my children have, though I love silence. Tonight, here in my room, something will come, I'm confident, the old music of my children outside my room; working music.

Carolyn Forché

> There is a kind of writer appearing with greater and greater frequency among us who witnesses the crimes of his own government against himself and his countrymen. He chooses to explore the intimate subject of a human being's relationship to the state. His is the universe of the imprisoned, the tortured, the disfigured, and the doleful authority for the truth of his work is usually his own body.... So let us propose discussion of the idea that a new art, with its own rules, is being generated in the twentieth century: the *Lieder* of victims of the state.
>
> —E.L. Doctorow, from a preface to *The Crowned Cannibals* by Reza Baraheni

¶

> ... a state is a human community that (successfully) claims the *monopoly of the legitimate use of physical force* within a given territory.... The state is considered the sole source of the "right" to use violence. Hence, "politics" for us means striving to share power or striving to influence the distribution of power, either among states or among groups within a state.... When a question is said to be a "political" question, when a cabinet minister or an official is said to be a "political" official, or when a decision is said to be "politically" determined, what is always meant is that interests in the distribution, maintenance, or transfer of power are decisive for answering the questions and determining the decision or the official's sphere of activity.... The state is a relation of men dominating men, a relation supported by means of legitimate (i.e. considered to be legitimate) violence.
>
> —Max Weber, "Politics as a Vocation"

These pages document an ongoing struggle within myself. They mark my attempt to conceive of a passionate and committed form of disinterest/universality.

¶

The assumption behind the critique of politics is that there is some realm which is never articulated—of common sense or the universal—

that is ahistorical, pre-political, and pre-social. The derivation of this is the natural law notion that people exist in the state of nature and they come together to form states. The humanism of the last two centuries, the educational humanism of the academy, has based itself and its authority on these eternal verities, specifically through the ideology of Arnoldianism from the late 1860s onwards. It sees its role as providing standards of excellence and eternal truths, which lead the mind out of its particular interests, toward the general interests of humanity, the generalizable interests, which are the interests of the ruling group at any one time. This can be seen in the interpretations of the Aeneid for the last one hundred and fifty years. What was taken in the 1880s as the great epic of empire, teaching Englishmen and Americans how to administer, became in the 1960s the great anti-imperialist epic.

In the twentieth century the social and the political have become so intertwined that it is very hard to distinguish them. There is poetry in the twentieth century that does not further a specific ideology, but engages the historical as a critique precisely of the incursions of politics into other forms of association. This poetry, while not political in the narrowest sense, is a protest against the violence perpetrated in the name of politics. Frequently, the critique will adopt the languages of religion, or of a humanistic, universalizing Marxism, especially when it is oppositional—that is to say, Marxism that has not come to power, or in the name of abstract notions like "justice." This poetry creates a public sphere in literature against the depredations of the private by the political, and situates itself in the realm of the social. It wants to use the affections of the private sphere as a way of critiquing the depredations of the political.

One would not want simply to relegate the poetry of witness to the public sphere, as it also situates itself in the intimate (private) and political realms ... Extremity marks the poetic imagination; one doesn't live through extreme conditions of this kind without being affected by them, and this mark appears in trace in the subsequent works, which can be read in light of what the author endured, whether or not the works explicitly address the experience.

Forché

(Lawrence) Langer identifies something he calls "wounded space." Memory is not only a spring, but also a tomb. He speaks at length about memory as excavation of a ruin, which reminds me of Benjamin. For the witness, he says, the Holocaust is "at once a lived event and a died event." Langer makes distinctions between kinds of memory: tainted, anguished, humiliated. He identifies anguished memory as that which eliminates repose. It pits authenticity against logic, and the failure to connect these two undoes every model and code ...

¶

(Hannah) Arendt is writing from the point of view of the person speaking. She is interested in the person's speaking and his or her integrity. (Ludwig) Wittgenstein is arguing against epistemology. He's not arguing about the person speaking, but those who are listening. He's saying that those listening have no reason to doubt pain, because pain cannot be known by another person; it can be expressed by pointing or groaning, but there are no criteria for knowledge. His argument is not an argument against skepticism, but that there are moments when the skeptical argument has no place. Arendt and (Elaine) Scarry are speaking existentially, and Wittgenstein is speaking as a philosopher trying to argue against the tyranny of epistemology, and the tyranny of certain notions of knowledge and falliblism. Why do I think Wittgenstein is right? All we have is language. And I know that I do not write from thoughts that already exist, but from thoughts that come to existence as they are inscribed. What would it mean to say that you have thoughts before you have language? Freud maintains that the unconscious is pre-linguistic, that there is no language in the unconscious, that it's only when things come to consciousness that they acquire language. So it might be true that we have thoughts that are pre-linguistic—however, *then* we are using the word "thought" for all mental processes, and that might be inaccurate. Conscious thought—how can you think a conscious thought that is not linguistic? Or is not shaped like a language? I don't think you can. So that's why I think that Wittgenstein is right. The emphasis is on looking at the words on the page, rather than trying to re-create a pre-existent thought that served as the motive force for

Forché

the words on the page. That frees us from the metaphysics of worrying about that which we cannot know, which is what the author intended to do. The author intended to *write*. In other words, the notion of intentionality is dissolved if you emphasize the words on the page.

¶

To argue completely against moments of nobility would be to concede everything to the dark time. One can celebrate the power of resistance to degradation without saying that degradation is productive. One sees in the nobility, in the moments of altruism, something that is very beautiful because hard won, without having then to sing paeans to the human spirit. The very human spirit that rises up in the concentration camps is also the human spirit that *created* the camps. Perhaps these separate issues are occluded when we speak about such generalized abstractions as "the human spirit." I think this is what Arendt tried to do in *Eichmann in Jerusalem*. In that book, Arendt's question is, "Why is it that some people become Nazis, and other people hide Jews?" There is nothing specifically altruistic about the human spirit. Rather, the three nations that saved the Jews, or tried to—Bulgarians, the Danes and the Italians—all did so for different reasons. The Danes because the Jews were citizens of Denmark, and they saw in the Jews fellow citizens. According to Arendt—and if her explanation is an interesting one politically for the Danes, it is somewhat feeble for the Italians (because of their "humanity" and three thousand years of civilization), and she has no idea why the Bulgarians did it. This is not a weakness on Arendt's part. In fact it is one of her strengths that she admits that when these things happen, they usually happen in groups, not in individuals. Arendt sees resistance as *contagious*, as she sees complicity. They are both contagious, and we don't know why.

There *is* a humanity toward which we aspire. Eichmann was unwilling to be *human*, that is to say, to live with other people. He was unwilling to accept alterity, which for Arendt is the definition of the human. Eichmann's pathology was a weak narcissism that couldn't imagine the alterity of others, and that's why he's given over completely to cliché.

Forché

Arendt's is a very strong form of existentialism. For her, to be "human" means to do two things—there are only two things that humans can do that other animals can't do: one is to persuade, and the other is to act, on the basis of that persuasion, and that for Arendt is the essence of politics. So that to be "human" is to live in non-violent political relations with other people. That is the *telos* of the human. For someone like Terrence (Des Pres), the "human" is a "God-term" which he doesn't define.

¶

How can we know another person's pain? I'll return tomorrow with arguments against even thinking about that question. Perhaps the word "know" means something different in the language game of epistemology and in the question of pain, or what happens in other minds. If I understand it correctly, one of the more interesting aspects of Wittgenstein's critique of metaphysics is that he shows that there are different meanings of the word "know," specifically in relation to pain. Stanley Cavell then proposes that, in fact, pain is not something that can be known, but only something that can be ac-*know*ledged. I must do more research on this. The arguments about whether you can know another's experience, or the claim made by witnesses that their experience is unknowable, avoids the issue of why it is we have witness in the first place. The literature of witness is one in which the questions concern authenticity and response, rather than knowledge, which is very different. The point is not whether the other persons *know* what this pain was, in other words "experience" it, but rather that they are forced into a position where they have to respond to it.

There is a problem in the question of testimony with the notion of literary language "expressing" extreme experience, and the distinction between this representation and the experience itself.

It is representation, but it's re-presentation, not re-experience. When you enter into the public sphere of writing, or the social sphere of poetry, what you are doing is demanding a response from the reader as much as attempting to re-create something that happened once.

> Man, pushed to the very limit of his condition, found once more in the written word a last rampart against the loneliness of annihilation. His words, elaborate or awkward, cadenced or disorderly, were inspired only by the will to express, to communicate, and to transmit truth. They were formulated in the worst conditions possible, were spread by impoverished means and dangerous by definition. Those words were opposed to the lie fabricated and maintained by powerful groups which had gigantic technology at their disposal and who were protected by unbounded violence.
> —Michal Borwicz, *Les Ecrits des condamnés à mort sous l'occupation allemande (1939–1945)*

These works *aren't* representational. I'll argue for the examination of witness as a *representational* mode of language as evidence, and as a way of thinking about repetition which is not governed by difference, but is founded upon a genuine sameness, that is, the original event *recurs* in the language present before us. I'm interested in the impress of extremity upon the poetic imagination and the ways in which these events incise consciousness.

> What the poem translates, I propose we call experience, on condition that this word be taken literally—from Latin, *experiri*: the risky crossing…, and this is why one can refer, strictly speaking, to a poetic existence, if existence it is that perforates a life and tears it, at times putting us beside ourselves.
> —Philippe Lacoue-Labarthe

This is where I find the trace, and this is where the event recurs. Witnesses beget witnesses. Evidence begets evidence. A poem by Celan is evidence of what happened to him.

> Writing leaves the trace of an original disaster which was not experienced in the first person precisely since it ruined this first person, reduced it to a ghostlike status, to being a 'me without me.'
> —Claire Nouvet, *An Impossible Response …*

Forché

> One thing remained attainable, close and unlost amidst all the losses: language.
>
> Language was not lost, in spite of all that happened. But it had to go through its own responselessness, go through horrible silences, go through the thousand darknesses of death-bringing speech. It went through and offered no words for what happened; but it went through these events ...
>
> I have attempted to write poems in this language, in those years and in the years that followed—in order to speak, in order to orient myself, in order to explore where I was and where I was yet to go, in order to define reality for myself.
>
> —Paul Celan, Bremen, 1958

¶

Perhaps the strength of deconstruction in America has been its demystification of very simplistic notions of representation, but, as Wittgenstein shows us, there are many different kinds of representation, and representation is not a fixed relation between two things that is already established, but one that keeps being re-established in new relations that aren't fixed. So that relation of word to world, to say that language doesn't express the world is, I think, primitive. I think this is using a very limited notion of representation in order to construct its paradoxes. In the end, language expresses everything that can be expressed. One of the great strengths of deconstruction and of modern philosophy and critical theory has been to make richer and more problematic our understanding of what representation *can* be, rather than seeing what representation *is*. I think this is important. The real wisdom of deconstruction is that it shows our notions of representation, and our representations to ourselves are in fact very rich. There are many different notions of how representation works, and many different notions of representation. And what might be necessary first is not to divide them into dichotomous binarisms, representational vs. non-representational, but say if all of this linguistic material is representational, then how does it work? In other words, *thick descriptions* of representations, rather than a realm of the non-representational. Although that is an important critical gesture, it keeps us locked in the binarism. It might be more interesting to say there are many different modes of representation, not all of them have the same relation to the reader, and not all have the same relation to whatever that thing is that we call experience.

¶

"The idea of mass graves seems to pertain especially to the twentieth century. There are two thousand five hundred British war cemeteries in France and Belgium. The sophisticated observer of rows of headstones will do well to suspect that very often the bodies below are buried in mass graves, with the headstones … in rows to convey the illusion that each soldier has his individual place." (Paul Fussel, *The Great War and Modern Memory*) This is an interesting point, and a painful one. There is a further distinction to be made between false mass graves that still resemble cemeteries, and mass graves that aren't even marked. Dachau. Auschwitz. The killing fields in Cambodia. And places we don't even know about. The point of mass graves is not memorialization. The military's war dead might have been buried together, but they are remembered as individuals. How different that is, say, from the mass graves outside Vilnius. These "non-people" were so completely massified that their individuation was lost completely. Fussell talks about the centrality of the notion of irony to our understanding of war as distinctly modern. It might be modern, but that irony is central as a *post-facto* way of viewing an event. It's only after you've gone through the event, or have some reason for the ironic re-description of the event that you can describe it ironically. Irony is a form of self-reflection, and can be effective if people are using the language that Fussell describes later, in his description of war in the terms set up not by Walter Scott, who thought war was hell, but by those who glorified it. In other words, the mock-Romanticism and the mock-Medievalism of the language of war. The language of going off to war in 1914 needed to be demystified. Irony was an important trope, but I wonder if it is a useful trope against war when war is perpetrated cynically. That is to say, when we know—when large numbers of the intelligentsia, the reading public, are cynical about war—as during the Vietnam War, or more importantly, as during

Forché

the Gulf War, when many were cynical about why we were doing this. Most knowledgeable people were of the view that the war was being fought for oil, that we weren't concerned with democracy in Kuwait, and a fair degree of cynicism was masked by our sheer excitement over the fact that techno-warfare "worked," and that the army did a "good job." But only the most benighted and the most unhappy, those who were fighting hardest against their cognitive dissonance, thought that the reasons for going to war were innocent. In that case, if one were being ironic, might not one be supporting the very cynicism that caused the war in the first place? That ironic distance is very important if you are going to demystify another language. But here the language was already demystifying itself: James Baker basically admitted that he could not find a good legitimation for this war when he first proposed that it would save American jobs, then changed tack to issue dire warnings about the Iraqi nuclear threat. We had to fall back on the notion of supporting our troops, rather than believing that we were fighting a just war. Even the political right acknowledged that it was probably an important war to fight, but not necessarily a just one, and not necessarily a moral one. If a war is fought cynically, then irony will not fight against the war, that in fact something else will have to, and that might be authenticity on one side, and a sense of cosmopolitanism …

¶

One of the dangers of irony, and ambiguity is merely another side of irony, is that you reinforce the status quo by stating that the situation is "ambiguous"—or you carve out a personal space of resistance through irony. In certain circumstances, a person's capacity for irony is very important, but I'm not sure it is sufficient. Most truth is ambiguous in that it requires very thick descriptions, but that does not mean that we must always take a distanced relation to circumstances in the hope that at some other time, or, metaphysically, in some other state of being, we might understand the truth a little better. "Right now it's too ambiguous. We can't make a move." The danger of that is obviously that you give the world over to those who have power, and you don't use the tremendous pathos and power of commitment and notions of truth, nor deploy the power that inheres in them against the power of violence, which is both the limit and the end of politics.

Fussell writes "simple antithesis everywhere, that is the atmosphere in which most poems of the Great War take place, and that is the reason for the failure of most of them as durable art." Understandably, he attacks melodramatic dichotomies. However, I wonder if perhaps—and this is where he gets more Johnsonian than he does new critical, that his notion of "durable" is a way of forgetting what Fussell wants us to remember: that war is specific, that it is horrible, that it happens to individuals. He's brilliant on the battle of Passiondael, whose name sounds like Waterloo, when in fact it wasn't a battle in the old fashioned sense at all, and it wasn't localized. If you could walk from the North Sea to the Swiss border and never come above ground, the notion of localization is no longer germane, because you're not moving with small mobile armies, but with large armies that are spread all over the map and fighting each other constantly. The notion of "durable art" might in fact miss the point of what is going on in this art. What he means by durable art is art that is ambiguous, that relishes ambiguity. I don't understand why that has to be the only durable form—he's using a Johnsonian notion and new critical criteria as a way of side-stepping the commitments of the art he's describing. His grand narrative of modernity is that the Great War marked our first fall into binary ideology, and what it did was solidify the notions of binary thought. The problem is that literary discourse, which is always seen as ironically more sophisticated and more naive than political discourse, falls into a form of petty adolescence or childhood when it tries to go cross into politics. Again, this is Fussell the New Critical ironist speaking. The difference between dialectics and binary forms of thought: dialectics are a way of thinking about a number of things at the same time. It's a mode of thought that allows you to *think* numerousness and heterogeneity. Binary thought, however, is one that keeps opposite poles opposite.

A way of understanding deconstruction and why deconstruction was so popular in the United States is that in many ways it was an introduction (especially in Paul de Man) to dialectical thought. Fussell quotes

Forché

Louis Simpson and he wants to refute him. Simpson maintains that language basically can't touch the body, the sheer physicality of a soldier's life can't be rendered into words. The reason is that soldiers have discovered that no one is really interested in the bad news they have to report. What listener wants to be torn and shaken when he doesn't have to be? We have made unspeakable mean indescribable. It really means "nasty." I think this is where Fussell's moralism and his hard empiricism are in fact accurate. To say that things are indescribable, that they leave language, is in fact to fall into the metaphysics that allows such things to happen again and again. They are not beyond language. They are not beyond communication. They are not beyond expression. To say that they are is to turn them into an event that doesn't happen and a death which doesn't touch us. It strikes me that it's this aspect of Heideggerian thought which is the most dangerous.

¶

Brooks and Warren's book on literature came out in '39—but it wasn't until *after* the war that new criticism really became institutionalized in the American academy. It was a perfect ideology for the cold war, because it stressed ambiguity, irony, and distance. It was a way of "freeing" oneself from ideology, which had become, after the war, understandably suspect. The ideologies of which they were suspect were essentially communism and fascism, and that is why the strength of new criticism and the particular domestications of deconstructionism can be found in the United States. De Man's deconstruction is a critique of the fascist temptation. When they discovered that he had been a minor collaborator during the Second World War, rather than claiming that this showed that deconstruction was tainted from the start, perhaps it showed that deconstruction was a very strong response. Look at the major deconstructionists: Derrida, a French Algerian Jew; Geoffrey Hartman, who was forced to flee Germany because he was a Jew, and de Man. There's a reason why they all came together on this, because they had all suffered, in one way or another, from excess of ideology.

¶

Forché

What I find significant about Berel Lang's work is his warning against writing about the subject of the Holocaust, or, as he'll later clarify, of the *Shoah*—unless one can add to the documentary knowledge something concrete, unless one discovers something new. And he talks about mediation of language and the position of the writer with respect to the material, and why one can't write about that event without taking many things into account. Then he talks about the distinction he makes between writing about the event and writing oneself, the writer writing him or herself in the present, through the event, and he likens that to the re-telling of the story of Exodus. This is precisely his answer to what the justification for writing about the Shoah is, the Haggadic stress on the eternal presence of God's actions for the Jewish people, that is to say, thus Adonai, the Lord, did for me when he brought me forth from Egypt—which is stressed several times in the Haggadah. So that in fact one writes oneself into it by placing oneself in relation to it, rather than it in relation to some great objectivity. One of the arguments in my book (*Against Forgetting: Twentieth Century Poetry of Witness*) is going to be against the notion of an enlightenment objectivity and an Archimedean stance outside of systems and outside of history. Lang seems to want to assert the *situatedness* of all knowledge, all responses and all events. The reason is that the moment of genocide is one that stresses specificity but also a certain kind of universality: "We are all humans, except for the Jews."

¶

> We were aware that the visible earth is made of ashes, and that ashes signify something.... And we see now that the abyss of history is deep enough to hold us all. We are aware that a civilization has the same fragility as a life.... Everything has not been lost, but everything has sensed that it might perish.
> —Paul Valéry, "The Crisis Of The Mind," 1919

Reginald Gibbons

1990

Poems don't "make" meaning (as if meaning were a product). What is the right metaphor? They leak it? Radiate it? What?

¶

"Magic realism" is the realistic presentation of what could never happen. Why not write "realistically" about what everyone knows did not happen?

¶

But who is it who writes this? It isn't me as I am during the day, either with others or alone, reading or writing. It is some other me, who almost, I would say, has no *right* to use my thoughts and feelings in this way. Who speaks, after some fashion, metaphorically, to hear his voice; who thinks to hear himself think. Not for the purpose, or not only for the purpose, of confessing, complaining, describing, recalling, etc., but also, and perhaps most, for the pleasure of creating himself as he goes. For the pleasure of existence—an existence which lies only here, in the pages written by me and by him. By him through me. I distance myself from myself even at the moment of my most unimpeded, unselfconscious scribbling.

We study literature (do we study literature?) because we find it pleasurable and edifying to pore over language in which there is a surplus of available meaning. (In this sense, only, is literature like religion: not a substitute but merely something analogous to holy writ, owning some analogous pleasures of mind—dispute, drama, narrative, etc.) And we also pore over literature because we like to "share consciousness." (Why do we like to do that?) And because reading poetry and fiction is much (most?) like the deep sharing of consciousness of lovers or intimates excited by each other's being. Seeing through each other's eyes. Objection: reading isn't reciprocal; the reader is at least relatively, and with some texts, very much, the passive figure who is led by the active author. Answer (besides the answer of pointing to works that ask the reader to be more than passive—starting with the explicit instructions in Cortazar's *Rayuela*): the experience of reading is not *reciprocal*, in the sense of conversation or even argument, but it is *mutual*, in the sense of shared observation, as by author and reader side by side. (And doesn't one, reading, sometimes see more than the author sees?) Of course the author points out and describes, but is only satisfied and fulfilled if the reader follows and observes also. And even questions—in which case the author may whisper: read again; or may remain silent.

¶

[In northern Wisconsin] At about six a.m., a raven flew croaking across the back yard, back in the trees. It was a striking sound. Then it flew back in the opposite direction, croaking again, and was gone. Shortly afterward a crow cawed, as if to have the last word, when the larger bird was gone.

¶

I write these sentences in this book because I don't want anyone to read them.

¶

The doorbell rang at nine p.m. I went down to open the door, puzzled. Without looking out the window first, and knowing I should have, but heedless to my own self-warning, I unlocked the door and swung it open. A young black man, looking very disturbed, asked me if I would give him seven dollars to rake the leaves to the curb—seven dollars so he could get his car started. "Rake them in the dark?" I asked. "I can see," he said. It was all too absurd, and the car preposterous, but danger overcame even reason. I opened my wallet and said to him, "Here's five," and he, thinking I meant to give him only that for raking them, said, "Oh, man." But I finished my sentence, giving him the five for nothing, and he said, "Thank you, chief," and I closed the door and locked it. And now am filled with apprehensiveness—not about him, but about life, all the wild danger in it: for us, for him, each of us a part of the danger to others.

¶

Gibbons

I woke remembering this slogan from a dream otherwise vanished:

> MAKE REVOLUTION OUR CULTURE
> MAKE CULTURE OUR REVOLUTION

¶

The Age of Waste

¶

1991

Playing the piano in the dark, empty chapel—under a very high ceiling, I could alternately listen to myself right over the keys, and then try to listen-from-afar, in that empty space. If I lifted my eyes up to the ceiling I could hear, listening-from-afar, what I was playing, instead of what I was thinking-to-play-while-playing. Something similar is required when one writes—to be able to listen-from-afar to one's words, as if in a large space. An empty church, especially if unlit, seems an especially good place to imagine (a Protestant church, especially one without ornament, or luxury, an architectural space, a space for human occupation that, with its high ceiling, frees the psyche to rise and reach outward).

¶

The parallelism and steady accretion of the language of Genesis, at least as the seventeenth century cast it into English, is as a gesture a *consoling*, however authoritative. One reads in a state of anticipatory grief. And the authority and consolation of Genesis comes from the syntactic structure, which with its simple parallelisms and repetitions is the language of an adult to a child. Since it is my present belief that poetry recovers and restores to us some of the language-use or language-repertoire of childhood, after force of mature habit has accustomed us too much to discursive and communicative or rather informational use of written language, it's no surprise that this first language or first text, Genesis, a text about firstness, is more like a "primitive" (and of course oral-tradition) use of language.

❡

January 15: Today an older white man gave C. an ugly sneer and the finger when he saw her antiwar sign in our car window. A recreational view of tragedy pervades the American culture—in a *New York Times* article today the responses of such people as tavern owners were presented—one, proprietor of a sports bar, said he had to put all his dozen huge TVs on the news and that the spectacle there was "fascinating" to him, "like a basketball game or a football game" because of the ticking clock. A war with a shot-clock—that will attract *lots* of American spectators, I do not doubt.

❡

January 16: Exhaustion and disaffection. The night the war was begun. Hundreds, thousands? of soldiers and civilians of Iraq, scheduled in secret and in advance to die on the 5:00 p.m. news. Bush on TV a few hours later, his face a mask of barely controlled hysteria, a glee of the melee, and the irreversible enormity, the decisive nihilistic feat. Even K., on the phone to her brother, was saying, "Did you hear Bush? He said innocent women and children were killed in Kuwait, and he's killing them himself in Iraq!" A miserable and morose night, followed by who knows what misery or how far-flung.

❡

January 17: In the hours of television I have watched, I've heard *one* person mention the deaths of Iraqis—an eighth-grade boy in a school classroom, where a ditsy and idiotic reporter pushed the microphone into a few young faces and asked for their feelings.

From Washington the smug and sycophantic White House television reporter keeps reporting on the *mood* of the President—he is "outraged" at Iraq's attacks, etc. *Why* should either government decisions or popular reaction hang on the moods of a lunatic?

Gibbons

Absurdities mount all day. One radio reporter said this afternoon that this was the first war in which active troops followed their own activity and made sense of it by the same continuous live broadcasts that people in this country were watching.

¶

January 31: First ground casualties of the war—including Marines who drove their vehicle the wrong way, made a wrong turn, into range of small arms fire from Iraqi troops—and did not hear fellow Marines calling to them, trying to warn them; and must have realized their mistake before they were shot and killed. Their commanding officer, interviewed on television, wept and turned away.

But no such weeping higher up; nor any for deaths of thousands on the other side. And thousands.

¶

A morning of false spring—warmth and sunlight. A woodpecker drumming nearby; sparrows chirping; three crows standing head to head in the church parking lot across the street, inspecting the gravel.

¶

February 23: The war on the ground was ordered and begun at about nine p.m. I wrote letters feverishly; paid bills; then began to work on a poem—a sorry collage, no doubt, but I can't do otherwise.... Yesterday a long line with many angles formed off of it, 2,000 geese perhaps, crossed the late afternoon sky with glorious honking and that—for me—overwhelmingly moving *striving* of their flight, fighting the wind. They are like horses racing. Flying W. by N.W. They must know that the winter will finish off milder, earlier than it has before. They must know this; or they'll all die.

¶

If I couldn't write—couldn't *make* something that by my own formation I understand, I believe, to be worthy and valuable, I would be able to live only for the sake of my efficiency at life's tasks—a hollow and wasted existence—especially so because I perceive no redeeming purpose handed *to* man. (But must I be so bleak—wouldn't it be possible to love, and to work for others? For right things?)

※

I read some of Cheever's journals in *The New Yorker*—the first batch of excerpts half a year ago or more, and was greatly drawn into them; then another long selection appeared a few months ago and these I did not finish, for despite the lovely accuracy and penetration of his brooding, the effect on me was of an elegant self-laceration prolonged and prolonged like a throbbing pain one almost enjoys. And I thought of how I could not write as well, nor wished to abrade my own self, scraping me till I bled, as he does.

※

I felt very *alone*. I was not lonely, I did not wish especially to be with anyone, I felt isolate, cut off from everything, I felt irredeemably individual.

※

The "homeless" do not constitute themselves as such, by that name. They are refugees and "homeless" in the sense associated with war and impoverishment, i.e., a "wandering." But we in this country attach another value to the word "homeless" when we apply it to them, and that is that they are not *owners*, it is "home" in the sense of "house" they don't have. Some of their advocates, I think I recall, have said they should be called "houseless," in order to provoke a material response to their needs. But in this country we so thoroughly conflate "house" with "home" that we do not see the other sense of "home" as readily as it is seen by peoples whose cultural traditions are tied to specific and relatively small locales.

In this sense, the extraordinary size of this country means that many of the population are culturally "homeless," their everyday existence includes no emotional attachment to a place because of its traditions or cultural inheritance—all American places look more and more alike, however sharply they may differ in real ways—ways underneath the surface, ways requiring subtle perceptiveness to be noticed.

❡

The companionable sound of sparrows outside the window—city birds, noisily squabbling or announcing in chirps their existence. A sound that comes into the upstairs room through the open window in summer.

❡

For much of my adult life I have wanted to be a writer; now I feel condemned to be one.

❡

Spoke with A. by phone, mentioned my next book of poems would be called simply *Odes* and all the poems in it would be about Richard Nixon. He laughed and wondered if it would be possible to amuse inveterate Nixon-haters (who, he said, were not *so* numerous) by rewriting the great poems, with Nixon in them: "Intimations of Nixon," etc. I would want to do *El cantar de mio Nixon*.

❡

On the airplane, a vegetarian eating his special lunch, reading a potboiler about Nazis.

❡

I have no mind for books today. A very smug, assured professor's voice comes through the wall of my office all morning, resounds down the hall—she leaves the door open so as to fill the whole space with her voice—as she lectures on imports and exports, currency rates, social security insurance, and other such matters. My office is unlit except by the window—it feels, seems, cooler thus. The extraordinary green of the trees, this time of year, fills the window, and from that direction, altho' not sufficient to answer the professor, comes the sound of sparrows, and traffic from Sheridan Road. And breezes, moving the leaves. All these books surrounding me here—a great *as if*. As if I were at home here, thinking, reading and writing. But instead I am sitting, in a kind of enforced state neither leisure nor work, a kind of busy procrastination, sitting amidst this extra hoard of papery possessions, my thoughts teeming with what has not yet been done at the same time I cannot say why I should do any of it except to satisfy myself, I cannot say whom any of it benefits except myself, as I leave my faint mark—Henry Miller said he wanted to leave a *scar* on the world!

Last week when I had lunch with H. we talked about his new book of poems, which I had just read in typescript, and liked best of all his work I've seen. We discovered each of us would like to do what the other has done—and which each of us feels is difficult or even impossible. For him, my *poemario*, so intricately orchestrated as he sees it, *mecanismo de relojeria* [a clockwork] he said. For me, the freedom and even excess of his book, the swift movement of it, darting here and there, without the restrictive hand of doubt on it. This from the man who doubted he'd ever write another poem—as he told me last year! I told him his collection was like someone's selected poems—each of the many sections giving the impression of being a selection from a complete book, so much *living* was in it, almost too much.

¶

V. told me that when someone [at a meeting to program literary events] proposed a poetry reading by cops who write poetry, another person said, "Yeah, and let's have a night for poets who beat people up."

¶

To transcribe from one's own journals gives one a posthumous feeling.

I wish I were here.

Allen Grossman

The Daily Bell Three Times Resounded

> But when hateful old age fastened fully upon him
> and he could not move or raise up any of his limbs
> this seemed to her in her heart to be the best plan:
> she placed him in a chamber and closed the shining doors.
> His voice flows on unending, but there is no strength,
> such as was present before, in his gnarled limbs.
>
> "Hymn to Aphrodite," 218–238
(transl. G. S. Kirk)

¶

1968

January 17: "The long schoolroom"—I take up this old notebook to remark that a teacher ought to be in a constant state of mourning. What is loved leaves him, and with perfect right.

> "Teach the woods and waters to lament"

The Cloud of Unknowing. The teacher's life is an undignified version of the *vita contemplativa*. Or it seems an extension of private experience. And, as such has, like sexual love, no legitimate access to public view. Still, my terror in writing about it.... Cheiron, who gave away his immortality.

¶

January 26: Pueblo incident. There is a stranger in the classroom always—ultimate audience, ultimate accuser. Students on a calliope or on a broad floor, sea of glass, who dance the dance of their authentic nature when the master is asleep.

¶

February 3: *lamentabile regnum* (*Aeneid*, II). Predicts use of tactical nuclear weapons in a month—Oracles of Zeus (Dodona, Olympia, Ammon). For what did we study? H.D.A. (drunk) calls all wives "brides." Questions why poetry cannot reach to the subject. Example of Matthiessen. "Bloody husband."

※

February 19: The problem with casual totalistic descriptions as educational tools is that they are not worth learning *in the way they are learned*. Anything underground is interesting.

※

February 21: *L'enfant abdique son extase.* (Mallarmé) Wisdom is not worth sightlessness. R. has no sense of possible futures. Battle for Hue continues. *koinonia*

※

February 22: Washington's Birthday. A man is a teacher by virtue of being something else.—The dark goddess with smothering wings—despair—the image buried under the threshold.

※

March 19: 40 hours of rain. *Sequere me* (the sleepwalker).

※

1983

May 10: Cold but brighter. Sun in room lights courtyard in picture.

※

May 11: Dark. Cold rain. Lilacs.

※

May 13: Dark. Mild. Dreams of an end: taking in lost children: tormenting slaves. The righteous grief of the Jews is one grief: there are others: pictures of the end. How does it end?

—The road seems to ascend toward a disturbed sea. Bisects an older road which is carried over it on a steel bridge.

※

May 17: Very fine. 9 AM, walked to bridge. Love: the single stone picked up by chance at the shore. You could keep it all your life, or one day, or one moment. Also you could have not seen it, as you did not see all the others.

"To understand your experience in order to contribute to the collective mastery of experience—that is to say, to *make* peace."

※

May 18: A fine day. *paulo maiora.*—Lady of the Lake.

※

May 19: Throne.

※

June 18: What was my father's thought? The threefold tablet: the one with clear marks, the one with unclear marks.... in the house of antiquities.

The sexual punishment of Carthage.

※

1990

June 17: Grasses. The wind blowing from the northwest has been upon the grasses all day—the grasses, blue clover and wild peas. The fog bank in shreds is driven—shreds and sleaves. The low tide is turned, and rising behind the veil, moving tremendously on its bed, preparing to rise again—rising—this time my death. The sound of it is from my left. On the right a river of fresh water runs from the land down to the sea bottom, down to the pit where the sea was, and will be.

—Building the ship with eight sails and fifty cannons.

"Hanoi—Former American and Vietnamese soldiers read poems to each other last week during an unprecedented writers' conference in this capital bombed by the United States during the Vietnam War."

¶

June 18: Big Tancook Island. What is a good word in America? What is a bad word? "Light reflected from water is always of the greatest interest."

Up and down the street they are struggling to make images which are right. But the images are not right.

¶

June 19:	SCIENTIA DONUM DEI EST
knowledge is a gift of God
UNDE VENDI NON POTEST
therefore it cannot be sold

To be penetrated by a dark myth, and leave it empty.

¶

June 20: "Whence and whither?"—Cattails. Glorious, self-possessed objects, bearing witness to quiet, pleasant days. *jeunesse dorée* 'With a light motion, and, as if by the sea shore, she said, "We must go on while it is still light."'

¶

June 22: "The sea is radiant," she says. One hears it on the short wave, "The sea is radiant." Then I say, "The sea is radiant." The sea is radiant.

THE SEA IS RADIANT

¶

June 23: "What are we doing here?" "We're on a journey, mother?" "We have to stop somewhere?" "Where can we stop in the heart of the hill country, the woods to the right and the woods to the left of us?"

¶

August: That he took your body from me was one death, but that he also intends to take your Jewish soul stops all thought in me which is the pride of life.

Rain has penetrated the book left in the open air like a dark myth, and it lies on the macadam the pages erased, the words gone under—and become again the dark element. The chamber is closed and closed the shining doors. My voice flows on unending but there is no strength in it such as was present before.

Donald Hall

August 22: Chemopoetics. The subject must begin with the grape, unless rhapsodes used other drugs. Chinese poets praise drunkenness; Horace writes hymns to wine. The grape is Dionysiac by convention but I doubt that myths arose without historical evidence. When do other drugs come in? Romantic opium and laudanum: DeQuincy, Coleridge with his self-medication, Baudelaire and the French. Now the tri-cyclics, Thorazine, MAO Inhibitors, Lithium, Prozac ...

Certainly in the sixties some poetry—not to mention endless prose—owed its manic rush to the laboratories of speed. Once Ted Berrigan stayed in my house for a while. All my pills disappeared: spansules supposedly for diet, pale orange Dexadrines that helped with hangovers. Ted apologized, faintly—excusing himself on account of the poems that zapped from these bottles. Some of his best things were those Ann Arbor elegies.

Reading late Auden, some of the poetry—and some essays in *The Dyer's Hand*—run on with a glib chattiness that reminds me of Dexamyl. Of course I'm not counting my current drugs of choice: black coffee and 5 a.m.

¶

September 5: A letter from somebody who likes a poem. Good. Somebody is out there. That's what the poetry reading is for—to prove that somebody is out there. When you publish in print, book or magazine, you cannot look in their eyes and see whether they are hearing you; they have to pick up a pen to tell you so. I remember the best fan mail. In 1983, I did a poem in a magazine, and a month later received an envelope addressed to me care of the magazine, forwarded; inside was a note, printed as if somebody had gone to private school, addressed "Dear Mr. Hall" and praising the poem. Folded into the unsigned piece of typing paper was a twenty dollar bill.

¶

September 20: Of making sports analogies the mucker knows no end. Never speak of proficient poets, without ideas or feelings, as "Good

Field No Hit." Never speak of vulnerability's superstars—loud with heartbreak, incapable of speech without cliché—as "No D."

¶

September 28: Flaubert said, "The idea springs from the form," which I prefer to "form is only the extension of content." The crafty Creeley said it but idiots quote it, to justify *Anything Goes*. The idea springs from the form because form *denies* ideas. Snodgrass said: By attending to form we occupy the surfaces of our minds, so that forbidden contents edge into the poem.

The Brothers Goncourt are critical. They complain that Flaubert went on "expounding with childish gravity and ridiculous solemnity ways of writing and rules for producing good prose. He attached so much importance to the clothing of an idea, to its color and material, that the idea became nothing but a pig on which to hang sound and light."

Emma Pig.

Flaubert quoted Buffon saying, "The manner in which a truth is enunciated is more useful to humanity than the truth itself." Maybe *The manner is the truth*.

¶

November 12: Writers as monsters. Victor Hugo carried a notebook in his pocket, not to write down what other people said, but to write down what *he* said. As he talked, if he said anything that interested him he took out his notebook.

¶

November 18: Pound declared that sperm was a cerebral fluid. Did he find this scientific information in Remy de Gourmont? Maybe in Balzac. The Goncourts claim that Balzac believed that "Sperms were an emission of cerebral matter and as it were a waste of creative power: and after one unfortunate incident, in the course of which he had forgotten his theories, he arrived at Latouche's exclaiming: 'I lost a book this morning.'"

❡

November 27: Bulletin from The War between the Poets and the Philosophers: David Antin: "if robert lowell is a poet i don't want to be a poet   if robert frost was a poet i don't want to be a poet   if socrates was a poet i'll consider it"

❡

November 28: There's a kind of poet (Sylvia Townsend Warner, Philip Whalen, Ted Berrigan) that one reads, not for words or phrases, or even single poems, but to make an acquaintance or to hear a pleasing voice. Frank O'Hara also. We become fond of the ambience, the sense of tone, the characteristic *turns*. When I admire Thomas Hardy or Ezra Pound or John Dryden, I try convincing you by saying a phrase, a line, a quatrain: I look you in the eye and say, "Here! Listen to this!" I can't do this with Berrigan; you have to steep yourself in O'Hara like tea.

❡

December 1: Heraclitus: "Opposition unites." "Men do not understand how that which draws apart agrees with itself; harmony lies in the bending back, as for instance of the bow and of the lyre." "One day is equal to every other." (Janice Joplin: "It's always the same fucking day.")

❡

December 13: Sydney Lanier on Walt Whitman: "As near as I can make it out, Whitman's argument seems to be that because a prairie is wide therefore debauchery is admirable, and because the Mississippi is long therefore every American is God."

❡

January 11: When you hear poets read their poems aloud, you needn't translate these sounds into the visual shape of the poem on the page;

imagination of visual shape is not part of listening, and it even distracts us—as when people try to follow a reading with an open book. On the other hand, when we read poetry in solitude and silence, the visual shape on the page helps us hear the poem. Or it should. Sometimes the shape has another separate function as decorative space—like lozenge-poems, or Herbert with his angel wings; these artifices give visual pleasure as well as being semantic—

but when contemporary poets drop and isolate a word—spacing it below a previous line, detaching it in a meadow of white—if our inward-voices do not learn to pick up this word and *hold* it, we make no connection between the visual and the audible. It should go without saying: When in silence and solitude we read poetry, if our throat does not become weary, either we read bad poetry or we read good poetry badly.

When Robert Creeley wrote "Poor. Old. Tired. Horse." he wrote something composite, amusing in its violation of propriety—and *also* something that we can imitate with our voice. We will pronounce it the way we would pronounce "poor old tired horse," but it is more pointed to look at: This pointedness is expressive …

Anselm Hollo

1979–1991

> "Lampshades! Lampshades!
> All sizes! All colors!
> Blue for comfort! Red for passion!
> Get yourselves a lampshade, Comrades!"
> —Mayakovsky, "The Bedbug"

Mina Loy the greater poet designed lampshades
(he writes these essays in his head)

¶

A great deal of *evasive* action in the "language-oriented" écriture: it's like trying to tell someone something without 'really' telling them … tease tease …

¶

Nobel prize to be divided in 3 equal parts between:
    h.c artmann (Austria)
    Paavo Haavikko (Finland)
    Ernesto Cardenal (Nicaragua)
            (conveyed to PEN 1-24-80)

¶

If you could find a large enough ocean to hold it,
Saturn would *float*
(radio info)

¶

music: people who really understand it must have a hard time in this (human, social) world—seeing, feeling, as they must, how terribly *skewed* that world is—in terms of over-all construction

¶

Hollo

"aesthetics
is for the artist
as ornithology
is for the birds"
—Barnett Newman

¶

re: "line breaks":
"She was speaking quietly but fast, and pausing for breath in the wrong places, the way politicians do when they fear interruption"
—Gavin Lyall ("The Crocus List")

¶

My tribe of poets isn't really "out for scars"
they'd much rather stay in their rooms
giggling over their notebooks

¶

"Satire
is an overloading of meaning
that so burdens the reader's belief
that it collapses,
exploding meaning
and hopefully leading it
in a direction opposite to
its stated intent"
—Daniel Gercke (Colorado Daily, 2-26-86)

¶

give me phrase or give me fable

¶

Hollo

Uninspired
today
my 'inspiration' is like Kit Robinson's cats:
First
they moved into the kitchen wall
Then
they were gone

※

guy looks like a giant molar with arms & legs

※

Je ne l'ai pas connu
Peter Whigham
but he sure was one hell of a translator
& not a mean poet
like his greatest past voice Catullus
perhaps even too kind
he came my way once
bewildered-bearded
silent & manic like so many of us

※

Ah, real estate ahoy! it is Columbus Day
the globe is still a globe, the paleface still holds sway
the buck's a buck, a slave's a slave—
etc.

※

"Anthologies are to poets as the zoo is to animals"
      —David Antin

※

Hollo

permanent diaspora—the ideal state
(my sympathies always with the Gypsies
rather than the Zionists or now Palestinians, etc.)

¶

writers of small language groups—their admirable stubbornness in clinging to the 'absoluteness' of their particular language—*their words*—by extension, that's of course true of everybody—

¶

"[critics] will always choose poetry which labors to be 'poetic,' whether by remembered forms or by a nostalgic, privately pained tilt of the head and vocal chords …"
                              —Marvin Bell

¶

re: translation as dealing-with-another-language—it can make you 'say' things you'd never 'say' in your 'own' language—i.e., not 'speech' in the sense that Robert Grenier dislikes it—more in the sense that he *writes* it

¶

what's feeble in (some) 'language-oriented' stuff is when it becomes these *bleak little exercises*

(or else when it expresses nothing as much as the need to exercise *control* over the work, *total*, if possible)

¶

Ezra Pound's complicated love life
drove him to Economics?

¶

Harper's Index—greatest American 'serial poem' of the Eighties

¶

Hollo

EP
just a cracker who fell in love with books

¶

All poetry is 'hermetic,' 'cryptic,' heretical use of words—not to sell, not to instruct in skills designed to produce & sell—so, in that sense, l'art is always pour l'art: the un-paraphrasable is what we want

¶

when "straight talk" was shown to be crooked
& "sincerity" merely as in "yours sincerely"
we got l=a=n=g=u=a=g=e

¶

"Dolphins (as we speak)
are carrying on 2
conversations simultaneously

& within the clicks of one
lie the squeaks of the other

they are alive in their little wandering pool"
    —Ted Berrigan & Anne Waldman ("Memorial Day")

¶

Le style pompier—the poetry of pompous statement—what *everybody*, from post-WW 2 Vienna School to the l=a=n=gs has been trying to get away from; yet these 'elevated diction' folks (mostly white Southern, in these States) keep cropping up …

¶

"We're all toast, anyway"
  —dude at Brigham Young University, to Jane, re: radiation hazards

¶

Hollo

Translations—often, perhaps always? at least partial mis-hearings—
what happens to every poem when someone else reads it

¶

the "Mac" put Tzara's instructions for Dada poem in "scrapbook"
(can't recall telling it to do so)

¶

"post-national"
(je suis)
but also "lower-case american"

¶

"I cut the orange in two, and couldn't make the two parts equal.
To which was I unjust? I'm going to eat them both!"
            —Alberto Caeiro (Fernando Pessoa)

¶

attention exactly *between* the words

¶

"No provision for transvestites in Geneva Convention"
"OK—put 'em in a separate tent"
            —News, Panama, January '90

¶

The "joys of opacity"—still a post-romantic yearning for
"l'innommable"—but Samuel Beckett (now gone) did it better: he's
never "opaque"—& he's still the champ

¶

'history' understood as "tales of the tribe"—nothing but an incitement
to endless *revenge*—maybe only those who are truly 'mixed' & 'exiled'
can step outside it: I come from at least 5 pairs of "arch enemies"—

Hollo

Finn/Swede, Finn/Russ, German/Pole, Pole/Russ, Russ/Germ—etc. etc., the gods know how it multiplies back & back …

¶

troubadour tradition: *oppositional* to patriarchal 'mainstream' (even if 'sexist' 'pedestalist' etc.)

¶

getting old when you start noticing how almost impossibly hard the young find it to be anywhere "on time"

¶

few notes, many poems
(the ideal state of affairs)

¶

the unbelievable badness of the well-intentioned

¶

"He could play a tomato can and make it sound good"
                        —Red Rodney, on Charlie Parker

¶

"signage"—buzzword at librarians' conference—means "to put up signs," like "No Eating"

¶

"what happened between the time he wrote those *nice* poems … and …"

Garrett Hongo

1982

October 1: Balboa. There's something like an "imaginative will"—a desire to exercise the mind, to use the imagination, a wish to conjure worlds of one's imagining simply to enjoy the task of that imagining. It's fun to tell stories, so we tell them. Wolf tickets sold not for profit but for the gain of the feelings they inspire.

¶

This is what the theorists mean, when they talk about the "repose of the imagination." The self-contemplative ideal that Flaubert is sometimes said to have invented, that Stephen Daedalus endorses and improves upon in *Portrait of the Artist as a Young Man*.

This is why so many of us prefer to live in these worlds of our own design—the idea of the poetic retreat, "Peter Quince at the Klavier," Kamo-no-Chōmei in his hut ten-foot square, Kenkō in his idleness, and Bashō in his unreal dwelling. I'm told that Pope had a fabulous garden to which he'd retire to write his caustic verse epistles. Whether he really did or not I'm not sure, being no scholar, but I am sure that he had a bower of sorts within the territory of his own poems. It was probably more pleasant for him than in society.

The Chinese have a word for poet that means "sorcerer" or "magician," but it also means "hermit." The notion contains within it an idea of the poet as alchemist of the human spirit, poetry as a kind of spiritual pharmaceutical.

But society still remains and so does the world. What can poems do for them? I'm fairly Confucian about this question and believe that if poems can order our thinking and inspire noble emotions within us, then in doing these things, they indirectly help the world. Poems inspire *jen*, a kind of metaphysical propriety and liberation within us that we need to keep going, maintain a generous-minded social equilibrium that can carry us through most of what's menial and trivial in our daily routines. Like the song says, "You gotta have heart!" and good poems, like good songs, restore that in us. *Kokoro*, the Japanese say, the life spirit. Love.

❡

> *But love is so hard here*
> *it has to be carved into a tree.*
> —Lance Patigian

❡

October 8: The world's body has been denied us. I want it back. And I use the erotic resonance of that metaphor purposefully because it is precisely that strong physical relationship with the world that modern, particularly modern urban, life seems to deny us. Poetry is my way of re-establishing that relationship, recapturing that lost love. It's a hermeneutic desire.

For Japanese Americans, the past is a corpse, a dead and foul thing we have all either avoided or been shielded from. Because of the circumstances of our history and its conjunction with a perhaps necessarily stoic psychological culture, the past has been something to be ashamed of and overcome, forgotten. I want to go into this territory of our dead, make them speak and reveal to me their emotional lives still unaccounted for. I'd like to spend my time listening to these ghosts, learning what I can of the circumstances of their lives—the immigration and early settlement, WWII and Relocation, the post-war return—and tell about them in a book of poems.

I propose to enter these lives through the study of documents and oral histories.

It's my way of bringing back what John Crowe Ransom called "the world's body."

❡

Hongo

October 17: What the Derrideans seem to want is the freedom to read a text in the same way as a poet "reads" the world—for the play of signifiers it "engenders" in their own texts.

❡

1984

June 23: Eugene. Seems to me the most beautiful, sentimental, and extravagant of all arts must be the hand-gestures of the hula ...

❡

The "Romantic Image" is simply a tool for emotional concentration and the release of emotion and a more complex imagery towards the making of a symbolic pattern that *has* emotion in it (i.e., that inspires and not merely "stands for" emotion). Yeats made it a craft and a discipline because of his needs and his background—his aesthetic roots in Pre-Raphaelite painting and an ideal of craftsmanship that must have been born partly out of a nativist pride, partly out of an atavistic affection for things Greek—"of hammered gold and gold enameling...."

❡

The trick is to make the memory, (or) the *imagined* experience, stronger than anything else in one's consciousness, to make the "pretend game" the one that counts, that is the death trap. Tricks of the mystics and the contemplatives should prove handy: simplify one's life; spend lots of time in solitude; avoid chaotic, undisciplined experiences until one is prepared to encounter them; quell the violent passions (jealousy, envy, malice). I'd add one dictum probably not present in any handbook for contemplatives—cultivate a refined sensuousness. Lots of the great and the near-great did this—one has only to think of Monet's gardens at Giverny, Neruda's study full of vari-colored, beach-scavenged bottles, ships-in-bottles, conch shells, and that sea-siren Madonna he scrounged and subsequently enshrined near his desk. Wordsworth had the entire Wye Valley, Frost his New Hampshire farm, Jeffers Tor House, Yeats his tower in Coole Park or Ballylee.

One of my most profound regrets is that I don't have a proper portrait of my father. I wonder—could I get a snapshot somehow and ask Wakako to paint one for my study?

Or could I imagine one myself? Paint it, "with poetry" as it were?

I remember a service picture, not a formal one, but a studio group portrait of three G.I.s in uniform, one of them my father. I seem to remember they had leis and big grins on, a stripe or two each, and service decorations. And except for being sepia-toned, the print was untinted.

What was lost?—those sparkling moments of clear emotion and generousness in the past, heirlooms of consciousness.

Returning vets, conquering heroes, 18 or 19 years old ...

¶

Worry is a mental erosion, a disease like leprosy upon consciousness, contagious and ultimately, to the imagination, fatal.

¶

1985

January 14: Columbia. Reading Robert Morgan's poems, I realize that my instincts are quite conservative in terms of poetic value—
    richness of diction and imagery
    strong, straight } crafted narrative
    a vanished thing set down in
        language the goal—this
           seems Frostian somehow,
              perhaps Yankee,
    though I can call up similarities to Japanese & Chinese
        poetry—
           Tsurayuki's *Preface*
           T'ao Ch'ien's poems for wine & friendship

My early teachers were conservative too in terms of their literary values— Bert Meyers, Stanley Crouch, and John Haines. They wanted a fairly straightforward and simplified diction, an elegance or stateliness of *tone*, and startling or even sometimes dazzling imagery and metaphor. Ideas were restricted to the aesthetic or the chthonic, a certain kind of primitivism the force behind much of this, with radical politics thrown in as spice, conscience, and Utopian dream.

Coherence, literary and political and emotional, was above all the guiding principle—a hatred of cultural and spiritual atavism.

Derrida in his critique of Kant and Hegel attacks this as a desire for religion, their philosophies a kind of secular theology smuggling back deism in what purports to be a rational philosophy, irrational desire masquerading in the rhetorical robes of dialectical reason.

Poetry, for my teachers, conducted no such masquerade. Rather, it declared itself as heir to the role religion might have served in more coherent societies, ritual might have performed in primitive cultures.

¶

June 27: Volcano. I guess it's true—my problem is a chronic one, that consciously and unconsciously *I make myself cultureless because of an internalized oppression*. I try to fit in with my surroundings to the point that I repress the better nature within, eliminate the Hawaiian, ghetto L.A., and Japanese roots.

There is nobility in these ways, there is a good and strong side to these impulses I should try to learn to tap into and restore so that I can maintain myself better as a healthy and creative psyche.

Here in Volcano, I feel like I've found the real thing again, found *my own way* and I'm not so worried about being competitive so long as I can always come from myself, so long as the poems can come from that better part of me so I breathe easy when I write, reach out to all the best parts of memory and imagination.

¶

July 6: Kawela. C. says that what I *wish* I could be is a "folk" artist the way Lau is or say, someone actually genuine. But the reality is I can't be that since I don't come out of an intact, received tradition but needed to construct my own art, amalgamating elements and influences eclectically, choosing and absorbing from pop culture, high art and literature, and a smattering of learning in Oriental studies. Not even the folklorist that Yeats or Synge were, the scholar that Snyder and Merwin are, I've had to freeboot, wildcat, and jerry-rig my practice together as Simon Rodia did his towers, Mingus did his music.

❦

Writerly riches are like vast landholdings—rent comes in from everywhere and you can inhabit what parcels you choose, when you choose. If you have a village, a kingdom, that you write from and about, you are wealthy to the point of embarrassment. *Material.* Rich in material. Faulkner, Garcia Marquez, Hardy.

[I write this 500 yds. from where my Kubota grandfather died in a state nursing home on Kamehameha Highway. I write this 2 miles from the sugar mill, surrounded by canefields where two generations of my family worked as laborers, where they owned nothing, not even the shacks they lived in.]

❦

August 6: Eugene. Poetry is a funny, appealing life. What it does I think is allow me to try to live as rich an emotional life as I can, mark passing events with a few words of the proper solemnity, speak as if I were writing letters to home to someone like my wife. Poetry ritualizes the emotions, makes, in the words of Grotowski, a kind of poor theater out of them, gives them a small public spectacle so that they can appear and be honored.

Donald Justice

HE [seizing her hands]: My, how cold your hands are!
SHE: I've been turning the ice-cream freezer.

¶

MOZART: Tears are the dominant my death resolves,
        Death being tonic for the Christian.
                [After reading the Turner biography]

¶

O attic solitudes! O clouds
All afternoon becalmed and ~~pure!~~   near

¶

Faust: A Skit
Narcissus: A Dialogue

¶

1974

July 7: Idea for play. Death of a Poet. Lorca in California. Time: 1999. Reagan has been governor for generations. Orange groves, guitars, motorcycles.

"Like a moonscape paved": how California looks now.

Full of broad half-deserted freeways, up and down which bands of helmeted motorcyclists cruise.

Of Los Angeles, crumbled by a succession of earthquakes: "Oh, yes, we could rebuild it, but what would be the use?"

"Was it not a judgment of God? Were not the sins manifest, and the sinners very great?"

Squatters on the ruins—families live in tents on the hill bearing the name Hollywood—and of them this observation: "Who knows? They may be the pioneers of the future. The Ninety-Niners."

Justice

Name of political party or movement? "Don't you think Fascism is a pretty used-up term?"

Song of the State Troopers

Blue are the cycles,
Dark blue the helmets.
The blue sleeves shine
With the rainbows of oil-slicks,
And why they don't cry is
Their hearts are leather,
Their skulls are hard plastic.

They come up the roads.
By night they come,
Hunched over headlamps,
Leaving behind them
A silence of rubber
And small fears like beach-sand
Ground underheel.
Look, concealed by their helmets
A vague outline
Of pistols is forming.
They go by—let them pass!

O town of the moonflower,
Preserve of the orange
And the burst guava,
Let them pass!

Song of the Hours

Three cyclists pass under
Christina's window.
How far out she leans!
But tonight she ignores
The flowering goggles.

Justice

Tonight she sees nothing
Of fumes, of bandanas.
And the breeze of eight-thirty
Comes fumbling the curtain,
Clumsy, uncertain.
    [PAUSE: *guitar chord*.]
O, the scent of the lemons!

Two hikers pass under
Christina's window.
How far out she leans!
But tonight she ignores
The bronze of their torsos.
Tonight she hears nothing
Of radios, of sirens.
And the breeze of nine-thirty
Encircles her waist.
How cool it is, how chaste!
    [PAUSE: *guitar chord*.]
O, the bitter groves!

A young man stands under
Christina's window.
How far out she leans!
But tonight she ignores
The shadow in shadow.
She sees and hears nothing
But the night, the dark night.
And the breeze of ten-thirty
Comes up from the south,
Hot breath on her mouth.
    [PAUSE: *guitar chord*.]
O, the teeth of their branches!

¶

F.S. FLINT: I have never yet heard verse read in any way pleasing to me except perhaps Miss Florence Farr's speaking to Psaltery of W.B. Yeats's verse.

¶

1980

December 12:

I think I could forgive you almost everything,
If you were here.
That way you had of speaking just too softly,
An act of aggression, really—
Now I would bend to catch your words
Without objecting or complaining.

And I can hear your voice repeating again the names of the heroes,
For there were always heroes—
Hemingway, Franz Kline, Bird, Ché—
And your voice naming them over is that of a king's
Elevating commoners,
Or that of an old astronomer naming stars.

There is a light that reaches us only after a long time.

Dust, dust, and a few lines mortal and evanescent.

¶

DAUGHTER: You're smiling, Father.
ST. JOHN: What, me?

ST. JOHN: But one doesn't have to know much theology to become an atheist.

> Awful writer! He makes his characters speak bad English, and they are no more aware of it than he is, poor fellows.

> Appearances go quite deep enough for me. Get appearances right and the rest follows. Distrust the profound.

Like James, I adore adverbs. Immensely.

I never lose my temper unless someone does something to annoy me!

We are old, yes, when we begin to tell ourselves that we are not.

❡

ST. JOHN: Look at the abyss long enough and it looks right back at you. *It's* not afraid.
FRIEND: That's Nietzsche, isn't it?
ST. JOHN [grudgingly]: It may be.

❡

1983

October 13: Once you turned off Ocean Drive you felt the difference. The sun was no less dazzling down those side streets, but it was no longer welcomed. Old people sat behind drawn Venetian blinds, diminutive fans turning. In the heat of the afternoon nothing moved. Cats slept in the shade of shrubs and occasional great tree roots. Once I stopped to watch a train of ants maneuvering torpidly across the pink stucco of a storefront, spelling out in insect hieroglyphics some cryptic message. Probably a warning about the future.

The moon shining on the sidewalk looked like snow.

It was a chilly morning for Miami Beach, and Levin wore an old yellow cardigan for warmth. Every half hour or so he would unbutton another button. The sweater had begun the day buttoned all the way up; now only one or two buttons remained to be loosened.

I stood behind the desk and lighted a king-sized Pall Mall. The classic brands were just then coming back after the war.

Everything looked worn-out and old, but to me it all seemed new and strange.

Justice

A short flagstone path halted at a plaster birdbath, dry now but still green with an ancient slime. Beside it there was an unoccupied stone bench. I say unoccupied because in all the months I worked at the hotel I never saw anyone sitting there. Once I did see an abandoned newspaper lying on it.

The only younger people we had all season were the two criminals.

Levin waited. At last he said, "I had a letter from my daughter. She has decided against coming down this winter."

¶

RILKE [Good Friday, 1913]: What, oh what would have to happen to me so that I might feel it?

¶

1984

February 15: In early middle age Eugene takes on a pupil different from the others—more talented. Other pupils strange in all the usual ways—wild eyes, wild habits, etc.—but the new pupil is strange in being so ordinary, except for his exceptional musical gifts. He seems as much interested in going into the family business (laundries?) as into music. And this bourgeois youth is so much more talented than the others that Eugene is both baffled and amused. Finally, the young man turns down a first-rate scholarship—and after awhile Eugene sees him no more—or only perhaps at an occasional concert or recital, with his family—eventually with wife and child. The former pupil seems quite happy, free of any regret. But Eugene himself cannot escape a feeling of deep regret whenever he encounters his former pupil.

¶

A room at the back of the house I was born in—the sleeping porch, with its tarpaulin blinds. Out behind, with blinds rolled up, a huge Australian pine, some oleanders, a sandy yard. Boarders slept in that room, sometimes a boarding uncle. I accompanied my mother into the room when she cleaned it. A mysterious semi-darkness in there with

Justice

the blinds down. Once an open suitcase, partially packed or partially unpacked, lying on the bed.

❡

Illustrations in the book of French fairy tales (Art Nouveau?) given me by next-door neighbor, a Mrs. Roland—her husband a policeman on the vice squad—would ride his motorcycle home and lean it casually in the portecochère. A gift of Bacardi from the Rolands (Prohibition still in effect)—contents poured out in back yard, the bottle used as doorstop. His suicide, involved in some scandal.

❡

Crossing the river from Georgia into Alabama—the summer my feet became the same size as my father's and I could wear his shoes (huaraches). The very thin sales-tax coin, almost weightless, representing one mill (I believe). *Oklahoma Kid* (Cagney and Bogart) on a Saturday night in the makeshift movie-house, probably in Dothan, the sepia tones of the print blended with the dust and heat and sweat of the night. Wooden benches.

❡

Florida (à la Henry James):
Here was the Infinite Previous—an age
When nothing yet was set down on the page,
A plate too primitive for all our inks,
A Nile before the Pharaoh or the Sphinx.

❡

Orpheus in Hell
It was a tropical landscape, much like Florida's, which he knew.
Childhood came blazing back at him. They glided across a black
And apathetic river which reflected nothing back,
Only his own face sinking gradually from view,

Justice

As in a fading photograph. There was no other cloud.
The trees applauded inwardly. Nothing was loud.
   . . .
He played a little on the King's piano, played Chopin.
   . . .
And everything became familiar as he sang.
   . . .
It was not possible to say just when he had begun
Departing, only that he was gone.
And that the landscape had continued on in him.

First person?

❡

A copy of Chekhov's stories lying open on a table. I realized all at once how glad I was that this man had lived. And that I did right to be glad.

Of what writers now could that honestly and simply be said? Take, for instance, Norman Mailer. Please.

❡

What does music mean? Stravinsky, who must be listened to, believed it meant nothing but itself. Obvious truth—for music does certainly mean itself if it is music. Can it mean anything beyond itself? Not the vulgar imitative stuff like the sheep bleating in Strauss. Not even the more refined imitation in baroque music when, following the verbal text, the voice-leading rises in hope or descends in despair.

That music which is most immediately rewarding—perhaps permanently so as well—often seems to behave *as if* it were referring to something, perhaps not presently known but ultimately knowable, if only … This has something to do with the ineffableness most people do actually feel in the presence of the greatest music.

Once in a while the listener does catch a hint of the Unexpressed. A possible example: the little triplet figure in bars 9 and 10 of Chopin's Nocturne in F Major, opus 15, number 1, and then repeated toward the end of the piece as the main theme returns:

Justice

What it would seem to be imitating, if anything, may be some brief utterance of, say, a languishing and rather pathetic ingenue, as she questions or perhaps resigns herself to fate. A poignant and brief sigh—trivial and familiar enough. But then, in addition, just underneath this pseudo-reference there seems to lurk another feeling, more hidden, not probably quite conscious on the composer's part. I want to suggest that in this little triplet figure we can catch—or almost catch—a premonition of the composer's early death; and I believe that a fleeting half awareness of this possibility contributes to the poignancy of the little moment. No doubt this notion will strike most readers as quite mad, at least when put as baldly as this. And yet ... why not? I have absolutely no wish to deny that the figure remains a triplet in notation and that the *musical* idea must have been primarily to effect a small and pleasing variation on the opening theme. The composer did often ornament the original statement of his themes, and with much more elaborate figures than this. Indeed, it is part of his signature, which here emerges as only a very modest flourish. That is, the music remains music and goes on meaning itself without interruption. And yet ...

Even Stravinsky allows for some translation of musical notation into statement or feeling, as when he distinguishes between Brahms's *lyrical* triplets and Mahler's *rhetorical* triplets. This much at least may be true: Chopin's triplets here are *very* lyrical, we may even say *poetical*, in that sense of the poetic we mean to invoke when speaking of anything but poetry itself and which has nothing to do with poetry.

¶

AUDEN [in a letter to a friend]: I've decided to go out in the New Year, as soon as the book is finished, to join the International Brigade in Spain. I so dislike everyday political activities that I don't do them, but here is something I can do as a citizen and not as a writer, and as I have no dependants [sic] I feel I ought to go; but, O, I do hope there are not too many surrealists there.

¶

Justice

Ah, ces banales
Musicales.

Of course they are absurd,
These little Bohemias of the suburbs.
And yet ... and yet ...

Wallflowers becalmed
Among the palms.

Society being merely prelude
To the final bliss of solitude.

A violin soaring upwards through Tschaikovsky,
Slightly off-key.

And cloudy afternoons
And organ-grinder (?) tunes.

How often, these Sunday afternoons,
One feels the desire for something different, less jejune.
Some thing both savage and ~~tragic~~, let us say ... / genuine

And there are times
Not all the gathered gloom of the sunken world
Can match the awful significance of one shaken curl.

It is this that ties the tongue in knots
And cannot be depended on or quite forgot.

Hearts in prison,
Slow-moving seasons.

Brisk strolls around the edges of a park—
Against the wind, bent, pursued by darkness.

The street lamp's halo:
A sudden glancing blow of yellow.

¶

Justice

Iris, and Jimmy the Greek, and beautiful Nancy Banks
Of Cleveland, hand in hand with Pony, her dark child—
Where are they now?
                        But we were talking jazz—
And Lady Day on a barstool once in the White Rose;
And that has got me brooding on the rose.

¶

MEZEY: It's a funny country, America. Success is even more dangerous than failure.

¶

O for a draft of Hemingway prose! His prose is "poetic"—and all this overwriting, mine included, is not. Of course Hemingway's is a type of overwriting too. One reason the old Constance Garnett translations remain the secret favorite of many, including me, is just that they *have* no style. Is that not, after all, the ideal condition?

¶

Why must I like it when they tell me my stories are "well written"? Of course they are! Would that this were not what they found to say about them, all the same. This ugly little piece of jargon seems to have become a code word for dull. Worse of course would be to hear that they were "well crafted."

¶

E.R. BURROUGHS: I am a very old man; how old I do not know.

X.J. Kennedy

1972–1978

Don't delay forever in writing your ambitious masterpiece. Recall that comic strip artist who drew "Happy Hooligan," the character with the tin can for a hat. By the time the poor fish had made enough money to quit drawing the strip, his hand was deformed, and all his attempts at Mona Lisas came out wearing tin cans like Happy Hooligan. I believe he committed suicide.

¶

Sometimes I wake in the middle of the night with good lines in my head. To go back to sleep, or get up and write them down? Recall what William Saroyan said: that if he'd got out of bed and written down all the good stuff he'd been too lazy to save, he would have been the greatest American writer. There's some use in keeping pencil and paper at bedside—and a small flashlight as a courtesy, if you don't sleep alone.

¶

To hell with poetry that has no more interest than the mere miserable prose meaning of it.

¶

People who distrust poetry but adore ideas always make much of the late poems of Stevens. Not that they're bad poetry, but they do attract a certain stripe of critic: brilliant, unplayful, and totally deaf to words.

¶

John Brinnin quotes a wonderful remark by William Carlos Williams: "I didn't go in for long lines because of my nervous nature."

¶

Kingsley Amis has pointed out that light verse is a parasite that feeds on serious poetry, can't live without it. So is open form poetry, which without traditional poetry would have no frame of reference. For their own survival, open form poets ought to pay us old formal geezers to keep writing. They need us as America needs England. (I'm thinking of

Karl Shapiro's poem praising the English: "Establish them, that values may go on.")

¶

Dylan Thomas has an appallingly ingenious poem of a hundred lines that rimes the first and last lines, then rimes lines 2 and 99, and so on down to a riming couplet in the middle: lines 50 and 51. Mike Fixler [Milton scholar teaching at Tufts] knows a name for this game and claims it's ancient. He says that Lamentations, the most heart-rending book in the Old Testament, is written in Hebrew as an alphabetical acrostic! Let them mull that who charge poets who write in strait forms with being insincere.

¶

The world is full of poets with languid wrenches who don't bother to take the last six turns on their bolts.

¶

The kind of reader I write for must be fast getting scarce: the reader who notices rhythms. Lately B.B., an intelligent bookstore proprietor, asked me where I'd got the form of the little short "Japanese Beetles"—he couldn't figure out whether they were inspired by haiku or tanka. He'd counted syllables and was puzzled to find ten to a line. So eye-minded was he, he'd never realized the things were in pentameter.

¶

Some critical fallacies that now prevail:

1. That confessional poets tell the truth about themselves. Hell, I'll bet the truth would be too piddling—they'd never admit how petty their foibles are, how humiliating. Of all the confessional poets who have confessed, does any deserve absolution?

2. That poets who have broken with traditional form are brave, daring, and original, while by implication those who continue to rime and scan are craven, lockstep imitators.

3. That the arrangement of poems in a book has sublime importance. Me, when I read a book, I don't give a hoot about how the poems are arranged; all that counts is: are there a few good poems in it? Auden once twitted this fallacy by arranging his *Collected Poems* by titles, in alphabetical order.

4. That beats placed with random irregularity can produce a *rhythm* (nervous, staccato, and therefore true to the pace of contemporary life). No rhythm can be produced except by repeating something.

5. That poetry should be obliged to mirror current events. (Guess that wipes out most of Herrick, Dickinson, John Clare, Roethke, etc.)

6. That a major poet is one who writes a new book every year.

¶

Josh (age 8): "How do lullabies work on babies? Do they bore them to sleep?"

¶

Woe's me—born just a little too late for the crest of formal poetry that rose in the 1950s, so that my stuff didn't begin to appear till the great stampede out of traditional form was on. So I came to the poetry scene like some guest who shows up just when the party is ending, the punch-bowl drained, the streamers all tromped to the floor.

¶

1984–1991

A gent in Houston, Loren D. Stark, sends an ad for a fascinating product that hits me as insane: *The Poets' Rhythm Dictionary*, designed to help poets find a word with the right rhythm. The first part of the book consists of 25,000 words in alphabetical order with "the correct rhythm symbol" marked on each word. I gather this would tell you nothing you couldn't find out from the diacritical marks in any dictionary. The second part of the book "lists the words under the correct symbol heading." O wow—if it has a heading for an iamb, what a hell of a lot of words must there be under it.

Now why is this notion so fug-headed? Intriguing to think why. I reckon (1) words in English do not have absolutely fixed rhythms when laid against a meter, else scansion would not be so subjective and controversial. (2) And who thinks first of rhythm? You say what you want to say. Say anything strong and say it well, and the rhythm takes care of itself.

¶

In Tucson, I met with students in a workshop taught by Jane Miller. One student had titled a poem "South Africa: For Nelson Mandela's 70th Birthday" and Miller objected to this title as too obvious. "Titles should be oblique," she declared. "They shouldn't tell us what the poem is *about*." I didn't see why they shouldn't. I like titles as obvious as billboards, myself—signs that point to the center of the poem. Especially if a poem is rich and complicated, hard for a reader to enter. Then, the reader casts about for any sign: which way to go in?

Jane Miller was a forthright, lively gadfly, and I liked her a lot. She took me to task for never writing in *open* form. Why didn't I try writing something that went against my nature, the way she and her students do when they write experimentally in meter? I said I couldn't do that. I like to stick to my nature. Pitiful though it may be, it's all I've got. (U. of Arizona, Nov. 15, 1988.)

¶

Has Wilbur's aim been low? Some—like Randall Jarrell, though he later changed his mind—say that Wilbur never takes large enough chances. His best works are short, and we, with our fondness for imposing edifices, prefer prodigious attempts, even failures like Thomas Wolfe's hippopotamine novels, which he himself couldn't complete, or like Hart Crane's grand and partially maudlin "Bridge." But the history of Wilbur's work is a history of successes—not vast, but modest successes, and they add up.

Has any historian of poetry ever realized that in poetry the successes are all that count? Most literary historians and seekers of dissertation topics look for epics—poems of colossal sweep, works of huge length and devouring ambition—and find Wilbur disappointing. He's been content, it seems, to let poems happen to him, content to render them in words as concise and inevitable as he can. For this reason, some critics will not grant him the epithet "great poet," a label that requires of its wearer efforts quite extraneous to the writing of poetry—efforts such as clasping the whole of America to one's beefy chest. Seen in this light, Emily Dickinson, that designer of brief lyrics, may not be so great a poet as Walt Whitman, not so ambitious and reportorial and encompassing. Yet when you compare her quality control with Walt's, she is certainly a hell of a lot more capable of writing poems.

¶

A competent formal poet thinks in cadences. Rhythm and sense arise at the same time.

¶

Warren Hope writing on James Reeves (in *Drastic Measures* Spring '88) says, "He once told me that he disliked great poets, preferring good poets on the ground that they are, 'Oh, so much *better*.' Greatness seemed to him a matter of mere size, goodness a matter of morality, of quality."

Half true. Great poets are also good poets (Dante, Yeats, Rilke, Milton), but there's sense in Reeves's remarks. Would-be great poets (Olson, Robert Duncan, Zukofsky) are only occasionally good, but indeed wonderful are those minor poets by whom we cherish only a handful of poems (Edward Thomas, Marvell, Clare, Louise Bogan, Stickney, Henry Reed &c).

Most of the factors that cause a poet to get into a history of poetry are quite irrelevant to poetry: things like significance, ideas, scope, the reflecting of cultural trends and forces, ambition and size of output, influences and personal associations with other poets, and so forth—

none of which has much to do with poetry. All a poem is is an emotionally disturbing structure made of words.

❡

Not sure, here in 1988, that we're enjoying a renaissance of rime and meter, as some claim. Magazines these days print a large number of formal poems embodying weak, moot feelings, cast into stanzas that look piled up laboriously. Today I browsed through proofs of an anthology of poems by high-school-age poets being published by Dick Lourie's leftwing Hanging Loose Press—they wanted a blurb out of me, of all people!—and raw stuff though it was, it was more fun and had more life to it than most formal poems I've seen lately.

❡

A long poem—how well is it put together? Easy to tell. A simple test: Do you need to turn the page to know you've come to its end?

❡

Bob Phillips, reviewing the *Selected Letters of John Crowe Ransom* in the NYTBR, quotes a choice Ransom remark: "Criticism is quite presumptuous, and I give it more and more reluctantly; I don't think it's quite a good man's business to do too much of it because it results in one of two ways: He commits gross injustices, or he is drawn too much out of his bias and nature by the effort of understanding and sympathy."

Those two faults dwell in practically all the reviews I've written. At a stroke, Ransom here explains my own customary unwillingness to review and my torments in the act of reviewing. I always feel that to write about someone's poetry is going to turn me into a wrongheaded bastard, or else into a silly grinner at anything mildly respectable. The only kind of poetry worth writing about is the kind naturally in tune with your own, which you approach with some zest, understanding, impassioned admiration, and a fair sense of its faults.

❡

Three cheers for any poet who handles words with the intent joy of a little kid playing with blocks.

¶

So many poets nowadays give us moral browbeatings. They imply that they confide things so intimate, so essential (to them, at least), that if we don't listen respectfully we are boors. Such poets often tell us about their childhoods and their spouses and their families. They're forever baring the secrets of the marriage bed, their awful or joyful confrontations with their children and their parents. Transfixed by looks of pain that seem to say, "Here's my heart, you bastard—you wouldn't dare stomp on it, would you?"—and we politely squirm, unable to run away. And yet we have every right to stomp on the unwanted gift of that heart, just as persons who receive, unasked for in the mail, junky crucifixes from monastic orders have a right to pitch them away.

William Matthews

"If we could know ourselves, it would be a violation of ourselves."
—Edwin Muir

¶

"*Tsar* and *Kaiser* are both cognates for *Caesar*," the Latin teacher tells students triumphantly. See how the past haunts us, the teacher means. A mob's a mob the world around, thinks a student. Why do people concur in these idolatries? What makes us like this? Why are we proud of it? Here's Leo Durocher in *Nice Guys Finish Last* (1975), telling us what a prince Frank Sinatra is by having God make this speech: "It's pretty dull up here today. Take a look down there and see what Francis is up to." Frank to the Reagans, Francis to God.

¶

"To eavesdrop is an ordeal."
—Elizabeth Bowen

¶

From a student paper on whether entertainers have an obligation to act as role models: "The reason young people don't respect their parents is they're not well known."

¶

Sebastian has sent me a tape from a new release of Bob Dylan bootlegs, so I spend a happy forty-five minutes comparing the versions of "Idiot Wind" I already have with one new to me. I envy the purely private fun it must be to turn one's work inside out, mock it, vamp it, make it both new and continuous with its former versions. A poem in a book is finished; the type is "set". I realize that I approach the "Selected" part of my oncoming "New & Selected Poems" with a gravedigger's melancholy but none of the gravedigger's nasty humor. The task feels like exhumation.

Years ago I went with James Alan McPherson to a diner for breakfast. He was then as shy and slow to speak in social life as he was eloquent at the desk. "How do you want your eggs?" the waitress asked. He thought and misfired on his first two answers. "Aw," he said, embarrassed, "fuck 'em up."

It has, I know, nothing to do with whether they're good or not, but I'd like the poems I'll select more if I could scramble them like that. Do I stand by them? Of course, even when that pose casts me as a gawky kid with a prom date. What did she see in him, or he in her? That's the wry investigation that Dylan gets to make.

Of course it's good to learn to read your poems as well as you can, but poetry is not performance. Poetry is writing.

¶

A journal is like a sketchbook, I guess. But suppose, instead of keeping one, I composed one, treating it as a rhetorical form with the same relationship to a working journal that an epistolary novel has to correspondence. Hmmm. "These fragments I have shored…" But not against ruins: what melancholy egotism that would be. The body isn't a ruin; it only ages. As the Kunitz poem has it, "I only rented this dust."

¶

I may well have on tape every recorded note played by Lester Young. The particles of musical information on each of those tapes are a sort of organized dust.

¶

"I need a rhythm section like old people need soft shoes," said Lester. They wheel it through the gates of the fort. Beautiful carving, beautiful wood. The Trojan Slipper.

¶

Half-rhymes: by rote, by heart. Dint, ain't. Tell, all. Finish, Spanish. Worse, Proust.

¶

In a bad end-rhymed poem, you can have 80% of the available fun by reading only the far right-hand strand of the poem, the beach where the vowels break, and there the plot, the argument, the "paraphrasable content" (but not the poem), the matter (but not the energy), are in swarm, like the bees in this morning's *Times*. The street (E. 82nd?) had to be closed off. Why were they there? "Apparently the queen had become attached to a white Honda."

In a good end-rhymed poem the bees are everywhere, but the rhymes help you know where you are. First *you* means the poet, and then the reader. There is no third person in this grammar.

¶

Soul: A reader? My kingdom for a reader.
Body: The reader can't come to the phone just now, but how about a mirror?

¶

Ali, after his loss to Holmes: "I had the world, and let me tell you, it wasn't nothing."

¶

Body: Why no poems in these notebooks, not even scraps or smithereens? What's the project, after all?
Soul: I'm going to ignore the moronic japery about the project. As for poems, there will be wine from these grapes.

¶

Some employees of the Federal Reserve Bank wear magnesium shoes to protect their toes against dropped gold ingots.

¶

Bread Loaf lecture coming up… How many odd rhetorical forms and feints I've devised over the years to avoid writing a conventional essay, in which, like a sheepdog, the author jollies along a flock of argument.

It's always a writer who thinks of himself as a realist, in the relationship he covets between his work and the texture of experience, who will say to me, quizzically, after I've read the piece, "It was fascinating, but what exactly did it mean?"

There's a rage for meaning, to be sure. Freud's work, in which every retrievable scrap of dream and slip of the tongue are wrung like precious sponges for meaning, may be the great, mad, tragic text on rage for meaning. What did he find? A blurry snapshot. So who benefits? We do, for we have his writings, a great emotional document.

¶

"Most of my life has been spent not understanding, and I can assure you, it was not easy."

—Rilke

¶

Freud, the gecko we bought to roam the apartment as an organic roach scourge, is visible, dully glued to the wall, after months as the stealth lizard. Did he wriggle along the pipes into apartments above or below us and come back for the water dish we faithfully set out for him, like milk and cookies for Santa? Where has he been? What does this sighting mean?

When Pat bought him, she asked the gecko vender what to feed him in case … umm … we ran out of roaches. There was a long Jack Benny pause.

Food? Water? Is he out because it's 98 degrees out there, fierce August in Manhattan, and where he ought to be (he's native to Africa) instead of here, this is weather he enjoys?

What does it mean? If we find him stiff and paws up on the kitchen floor one morning we'll really need a meaning, and we'll find it because the need is great. The rage for meaning is religious, but life isn't.

How did the gecko get his name? Betsy, eleven, saw a stuffed animal in FAO Schwartz sold as "Freud," no doubt because you can talk to it, like a shrink or imaginary friend, and not get a lot of backtalk. But it was impossibly expensive. Later that afternoon, Pat bought the gecko. What to call it? she murmured aloud.

"Freud!" said Betsy, dreamily.

¶

You can abandon your own poem at any point, not so much because it's done, but because 700 calories, or 7,000, of additional energy spent on it wouldn't produce, you judge, proportionate improvement. On to the next, you decide; they're your poems and it's your energy. And you're not done, either.

But Martial's been done since AD 104. What right do you have to abandon that epigram that even Dudley Fitts, or Rolfe Humphries, or James Michie, or Fiona Pitt-Keithley, didn't quite get right, or so you suspect the more strongly the longer you too fail to get it right?

You have every right. You're just a minnow and Martial's a mullet, but he's dead and you're not.

¶

Translation's a problem in English. In the first sentence of this year's Bread Loaf anti-lecture I use the word "gaud," but in my Southwestern Ohio dialect it will sound like "god," or, worse, "God," and in order to read it aloud without wrongly causing puzzlement or hurt I'll need to frontload, as the mutual fund salespeople say, the talk with an explanation.

¶

"It's all material, I know...," I heard a writer begin a sentence that listed a deluge of grief and death and betrayal that would make Job burst like a boil. Living in the material world …

It's pain. The meaning of pain is pain.

¶

"Regret is the fruit of pity."

—Genghis Khan

※

How private is a journal? Why would he say, for example, "Betsy, age eleven?" He knows how old she is. Who's this written for? What does it mean to sing in the shower? If a shower falls over on a desert island …?

※

If you write it, it's not private. Scholars and, of course, lawyers believe this. I once heard a lawyer, not mine, say, "It's our position that this piece of paper doesn't exist." Privacy can be like that, too.

※

> This is my curse. *Pompous*, I pray
> That you believe the things you say
> And that you live them day by day.
> —JV Cunningham

※

Epitaph: Was I right or what?

※

Sibelius, asked the meaning of his fourth symphony: "Play the record again."

※

"I think your poem doesn't take enough risks," one kind of workshop student will say. But nobody ought to be allowed to visit that kind of moral blackmail on a fellow student. The teacher should require the assailant to say exactly what kinds of risk, and exactly where in the poem they should be taken, and exactly where his gall and boorishness came from.

※

To get out of her house for a while, my grandmother asked me to take her for a drive around the small village she's lived in all but twenty of her ninety-five years. "The Lovetts' house once," she'd say. "No more."

Another house: "Martin Mortimer's place. Three wives."

"What was he like?" I asked.

"Dreadful snob," she said.

Another house. "Handsome Don Ransom's house," she said.

"What did he look like?"

"A chipmunk."

You get old, you hoard your verbs.

Of course if you were born in 1896, your world has shed its skin five times or six, and you're the oldest person you've actually met. When was the last time you dreamed of anyone still alive?

※

Rebuild. Retool. Remarry. Change your life. Do we index that last one under 'Life, you must change your,' or under 'Change your life, you must'? Or under both? Why, whenever I hear that half-line of Rilke quoted, always solemnly, do I wonder how large a diaper I'll need?

※

The detached raptures of gossip. Those who can, do, and those who can't, accuse? It's trickier than that.

※

Gossip: a way to inflict the sadness you fear on others. Or, sadder than that, the happiness.

※

Gossip is a larger truth than fact, but it isn't true about what it swears it's true about. Fiction is far more direct.

¶

The interest of gossip consists in how much work it takes, and how enjoyable that is, to change the known world to fit a theory about it. In that way, it's like reading detective fiction, or most literary criticism.

¶

Gossip: I know it's true; I heard it from you.
Art: You know it's true; you heard it from me.

¶

"It's important, that's what you mean, right?" one of my best students asked me last spring, and of course I must have thought that or why would I spend so slavishly and sloppily my passion on it? Of course I thought so, but was I right, or what? What did it mean? "Suppose it had no importance at all," I said, "except to you. Would you still do it? Pinball, scratchy historical opera records, ritual murder, differential calculus?"

"Oh God," they thought, and I could see them think it, the way you can see the wind in a wheatfield when it shifts direction, "here he goes again, keeping his courage up and hoping we'll think he's doing it for us."

1990

June 3: "They really be singing about the way they feel inside. Since they can't say it to nobody, they sing a song about it."
—prisoner in Texas about other inmates singing the blues

※

June 6: Saw a deer Monday night. Large animal steps out on the road. I slow down. It's a doe. Taking her time. Headlights of the car violate her vibrant darkness. She doesn't understand. Stops. But it's more than that. I know she wants me to see her. She raises her head. What? "Delicate body safe and whole." And she walks slowly off into the woods. The dog is barking up enough loud lumber to build a mansion so it is a noisy quiet moment. But neither the deer nor I pay much attention.

First drive-in theater started today in 1933.

"A poem," Robert Frost said, "assumes direction with the first line laid down ... runs a course of lucky events, and ends in a clarification of life—not necessarily a great clarification, such as sects ... are founded on, but in a momentary stay against confusion."

※

June 12: The rat is dead: the rat of industrial-strength pollution; the rat of toxic waste; the rat of rotten food; the rat of dump disease; the rat gnawing on a baby's leg; the rabid rat; the rat of no reprise is dead, killed by a pair of black scissors, sliced into a million insignificant pieces, paltry pieces, pieces of paper, the King of Rats now lying not even in a coffin nor in the filthy hallways of his underground kingdom. Just scraps in a wastebasket heading off to be burned in a Biddeford incinerator. Goodbye Mr. Scrap Metal Rat: Mr. Always Right Rat; Mr. Kill Children Rat; Mr. Lost on the Storm-Hidden Horizon Rat; Mr. Pull a Nasty Surprise Out of Your Pocket Rat; Mr. Kill Your Wife Rat. So long. Have a long rough trip to the incinerator. Remember what you did to deserve this death; for each scrap left of you, remember 1,000 times how full of happiness we are at your timely demise. Molester of children and soul-searer, so long, adieu, we won't be waving any tear-stained hankies at *you*.

¶

June 16: "It takes more energy to keep quiet than to speak your mind."
—Jamaican helicopter pilot
Day of the Dead

Thurs.? In Durham—I swear I saw what looked like a truck full of mummies. People all wrapped in white bandages, heaped one on top of each other, just like a museum haul, Egyptian section. What it *was* I don't know.

I leave Portland. D. looks heartbroken. The fog has spread from Portland all the way to Dover.

I feel like a zombie, so sad. So confused.

I eat a plate of noodles and watch Bette Davis die of a brain tumor in *Dark Victory*. I do not drink myself into a stupor. I do not drink. This is a victory and not a dark one either.

Received an invitation to attend the launch of the space shuttle Atlantis in November.

¶

July 1: Walking through Portsmouth with Sunshine the dog. Old guy walks up to me, says, "I wish I could be your dog."

"You do?" I ask, startled.

He repeats what he's just said. Then points back toward an old woman following him and says, "Yes, if I had lived my life as your dog, my life would have been a lot happier than the life I had *with her*."

She then passes me and says, in an even, loving voice, "His life has been full of pain …" and walks on. There is a small child tagging along behind her. I don't remember if it is a boy or a girl. Probably a little boy. And off they go. I don't know them, have never talked to them before. It is like an image from a dream and it happened.

¶

July 2: "Just because you're standing at the base of the cornucopia doesn't mean you are going to be killed by a flying grape."
                                                            —Gary Bromley

¶

July 26: little scissor pieces smoothed into the *who* who was first …
to leap from behind the one-way mirror …
to wear maple leaves pinned to your gloves …
to phone the giraffe at the zoo and say *You—who up there hello from my new blue shoes.*

¶

August 30: Show on Mother Theresa. For some reason, I always thought she was something like a milkweed seed floating around, gossamer and timid. But she's more like a tractor, going right in and doing what needs to be done. I felt like becoming one of her nuns while watching the show. It wore off. But her simplicity, her belief in love are tremendous. I can carry some of that into my life without cutting my hair and wearing white hoods. F. tells me I don't have the "mechanics" to be a Mother Theresa type. Not wired that way.

¶

August 31: Saw P. just back from Japan. Told me that while he was there he read a lot of Buddhism: "I found I could no longer kill things. Not even things biting me in the middle of the night, in the dark. I would just brush them off. Not even *cockroaches*. I don't believe in reincarnation. Nothing remotely like it. But I came to see that all life is more or less of equal significance. Isn't it?"

Yes.

¶

September 1: J. and I went to Jenness Beach and walked for awhile. Half moon making white roads to infinity on the lolling roll of ocean. Huge scatter of stars. The dog flying around connecting up pairs of strolling lovers the way the kid with the big pencil connects dots to make some sort of recognizable picture out of apparent dot-chaos.

Something at water's edge. "That a fish?" I ask J.

"No," he says, "it's a plastic bag" and goes to pick it up and it's a sand shark. He yells SHARK.

Moon-blue water. So many stars you know the soup will always be salted.

¶

September 5: Streamers. Confetti. The white ocean liner sailing for the moon. Spoons of moonlight to eat our peach sherbet with. Red monkeys—chink-chink-cheye-eye-eye singing in the red love-me trees. A wind of apples and white sails.

¶

September 8: By the time the water rose and touched me where I lay sleeping on a rock, I was ready to wake and knew it was no mistake that my leg stayed leg and did not sprout fin, no beryl-green tail. One plain white sail far at the edge of the world marked the difference between sky and sea. I woke wife to wind, married like sky-blue to water-blue, human woman, wanting to be able to take joy in. Without apology.

A good poem is like a strange room. You enter. The furniture is at once familiar and perfectly new. You sit down, a little afraid, but at ease. The windows. There are so many of them. The view from each one, shot through with an early evening light. Or it is dawn. Small animals slide through the room in their moderate shadows. If you want a lamp, then there is a lamp. If you do not, then it is dark. A red plum glows on the windowsill.

¶

September 10: Companion: literally "bread fellow"—one with whom you share bread.

¶

September 20:
"Think not because no man sees
Such things will remain unseen."
　　　　　—Longfellow

¶

September 21: Had a Mother Theresa party. R. likes "concepts". We're planning a Garbo party, too. Last night, R. and I dressed up as nuns. *She* had on a white sheet and truly looked like some very eccentric religious fanatic. She almost knocked on the neighbor's door, the VietNam vet. And I had to rush out in *my* robes to retrieve her. Cooked chicken in a sauce of fresh tomatoes, basil, mushrooms, onions, garlic, oregano. Brown rice. Asparagus. Then we watched the Mother Theresa video.

Right in the middle of this, TJ, a kid from some Florida college called. Because she was doing a poetry performance and was using "The Will to Live" and "Aubade."

A spunky girl who says, "I told my Mama and my family and my room-mates I was going to be calling a real author. I'm just *so* excited to be talking to a *real* writer." And I can hear her room-mate come in and say, "You talking to somebody *published*, girl?"

TJ said, "Mostly the poets I read are dead and I interpret them and my teachers tell me I'm wrong. So this teacher gives us all an anthology and says—these poets are all living and you've got to pick one for your project. So I said to myself, "I'm going to pick a poet and I'm going to *find* her. So I *did*."

She'd chosen "Will to Live" because it was gentle and "Aubade" because it was about lovers … Wanted to check with me to see if she'd figured out the poems correctly and was very happy that she and I saw the poems the same way. Said she could now use the author as back-up in case the teacher said she was wrong.

So there I am in my Mother Theresa costume talking to girl named TJ from Gainesville, Florida who loved my poems enough to find me, call me. One of life's grand moments.

¶

September 28:
When you lift fog
lift fog with your legs
not your back
    —someone said this on the radio

¶

October 4: There is a day when you notice that the birds are leaving and this is the day. A crow shepherds out the tiny pilgrims.

¶

October 17: If you are going to touch me it better be the way a ginkgo leaf touches nothing as it falls from the branch; the way rain is everywhere but cannot be put in prison; the way ink obeys the pen to form words; the way music makes itself known, the invisible city, that citizenship. Au coeur.

¶

October 18: Dream: *Max the cat has been eating all the bacon grease. When I catch a glimpse of him, I see he has picked up a spoon and though he maneuvers it awkwardly, he gets the spoon with the big lumps of grease into his mouth. He doesn't know I see him do this. I am delighted that I have a cat who secretly uses silverware.*

¶

October 20: cree-ate-iv-ity:
to make; to stop faking, to let the **be** be visible, to sew Sophie her coat; to write new poems, not just probing the red people in their cave but to be the wind in all the free red leaves leasing the cold streets. Ah! the strip teaser wraps her boa-feathers about her and struts off the stage. Sorry boys, she says, I'm going home to crack a few eggs, get the iron

skillet red as Pompeii and let my omelette rise. Not interested anymore in what comes off. Only in what it's made up of: green pepper, provolone, garlic, salt, sequins, cayenne, a little midnight, alot of what the white chicken dreamed as her feathers flew. Little egg come loose.

¶

October 22: "Some circumstantial evidence is very strong, as when you find a trout in the milk."
—Thoreau

Hundreds of sea gulls in an empty mall parking lot. They think it's the ocean. They are waiting for fish to rise up through the gray water. Hey, dummies! That isn't water. That's asphalt ...

¶

November 5: Cats turned blue in the attic window at the big white house on the corner. Owners watching T.V. Their cats, watching the night.

J. D. McClatchy

[I have from time to time kept both a notebook and a journal. They are very different things, as different as a recipe and the plat du jour. The one book I've scribbled in consistently, though, is my commonplace book, a sort of ledger of instructive pleasures. "By necessity, by proclivity,—and by delight, we all quote," says Emerson. But there is more to it than that. The sentences I hoard are—to be literally figurative about it—images. As G. K. Chesterton once wrote: "The original quality in any man of imagination is imagery. It is a thing like the landscape of his dreams; the sort of world he would like to make or in which he would wish to wander; the strange flora and fauna of his own secret planet; the sort of thing he likes to think about." The bower-bird in me is forever collecting colored threads and mirror-shards to make a sort of world. I don't use them in my poems; I steal from them for my prose. I collect to admire, not merely to appropriate them. Perhaps one day I shall make a small book of them. Fifteen years ago, I included aphorisms of my own. (Here's one that comes to hand: "Memory's like a cherished old neighborhood. After a time, the wrong sort of people move in.") I had lists of words that intrigued me; catalogues of "other voices overheard" while poems by Crane or Stevens or Warren were read out to me after a dose of hashish; lists of ideas from Wilde or Proust or Valéry; bits clipped from newspapers are tipped in. Nowadays, the entries are less frequent, more bemused, less intimate. There's a recurring character, named X, to whom phrases happen. What follows are a few excerpts, more or less randomly chosen.]

❡

"Those who have free seats boo first."

—Chinese saying

❡

Thoreau, in his Journals, on how hard it is to read a contemporary poet critically: "For, we are such a near and kind and knowing audience as he will never have again. We go within the fane of the temple, but posterity will have to stand without and consider the vast proportions and grandeur of the building."

❡

McClatchy

An example of literalism. When Lord Cornbury opened the New York Assembly in 1702 in drag—in the style of Queen Anne, in fact—and was challenged, he is reported to have answered: "You are all very stupid people not to see the propriety of it all. In this place, and on this occasion, I represent a woman, and in all respects I ought to represent her as faithfully as I can."

¶

—his squeeze-box
—but less of that anon

¶

"For the last third of life there remains only work. It alone is always stimulating, rejuvenating, exciting and satisfying."
—Käthe Kollwitz

¶

"When the axe came into the forest, the trees said: the handle is one of us."
—Turkish saying

¶

Apropos the work of older artists becoming more spare, it should be noted that this is not always obvious. *Parsifal* is the thinnest of RW's scores (in terms of printed bulk, that is).

¶

—*frère-ennemi*
bel canto > *can belto*
Eadweard Muybridge sequential photographs > Egyptian two-dimensional figures
—X's ideas seem to have been lifted from fortune cookies
—*limae labor* (Horace), "the work of the file"
—scrape X off my shoes
—*bougereauté*

¶

"All literature is to me me."
—G. Stein

¶

Van Eyk's motto: "As I can but not as I would."

¶

"Il faut choisir: une chose ne peut pas être à la fois vraie et vraisemble."
—Braque

¶

February 12, 1987: On Joyce Carol Oates' office door, she's taped up a card on which she's typed out this remark by Robt. Louis Stevenson: "To be idle requires a strong sense of personal identity."

¶

On the overemphasis of clarity in writing: A. J. Liebling said the only way to make clear pea soup is to leave out the peas.

¶

"Cinema is simply pieces of film put together in a manner that creates ideas and emotions."
—Hitchcock

¶

"Rome, Italy, is what happens when buildings last too long."
—Andy Warhol

¶

Ravel, on his critics: "Does it not occur to these people that I may be artificial by nature?"

¶

"Verse that is too easie is like the tale of a rosted horse."
—Gascoigne

¶

McClatchy

On a postcard from the old, ailing Auden to a composer who'd asked him for a libretto: "Too sad to sing."

☙

Hemingway said there are two ways to spend an evening. Get into your Buick, shut the windows and sit near the exhaust. Or go to a cocktail party.

☙

Frost said he was "content with the old-fashion way to be new."

☙

The story is told—I think of Brahms—that the master is made to listen to a new score by a young composer. As he did, he kept raising his hat. The young man asked him why. "I'm just saying hello to old friends," he replied.

☙

Told that a certain poem resembled an older poem, Allen Tate replied, "It had damn well better."

☙

Poussin, from a letter to a friend, 1642: "The beautiful girls you will have seen at Nîmes will not, I am certain, delight your spirits less than the sight of the beautiful columns of the Maison Carrée, since the latter are only ancient copies of the former."

☙

Fernando Pessoa's heteronyms: Alvaro de Campos, Ricardo Reis, Alberto Caeiro.

☙

hanami—[the season of] cherry blossom viewing.

☙

Which mandarin has the longest fingernails?
—bread and circuses
—X's work is like a Grinling Gibbons carving
—mutton dressed as lamb

※

Coleridge described himself as a "library-cormorant."

※

Poe distinguishes between obscurity of expression and the expression of obscurity.

※

Du Bellay: *"rien ne dure au monde que le tourment."*

※

Res tene, verba sequentur
       —Cato the Elder

※

Virgil Thomson, watching a beautiful woman walk toward him down Fifth Avenue, turned to his companion and whispered: "It's at times like this I wish I were … a lesbian."

※

Philip Sidney wanted from poetry a "heart-ravishing knowledge."

※

Mallarmé said that the French word for "day" sounded like night, and vice versa.

※

"Who plans suicide sitting in the sun?"
       —Elizabeth Smart

※

McClatchy

The Marquis de Sade is descended from the same family as Petrarch's Laura.

¶

Paul noticed this bumper sticker on the LA Freeway yesterday: "The meek are contesting the will."

¶

—*sottocapi*
—X is copperbottoming his career
—The Flat Earth Society

¶

Dylan Thomas's blurb for Flann O'Brien's *At Swim-Two-Birds*: "This is just the book to give your sister if she's a loud, dirty, boozy girl."

¶

On his passport, Stravinsky listed himself as "inventor of sounds."

¶

Maria Tallchief, withdrawing from the New York City Ballet in 1965: "I don't mind being listed alphabetically, but I do mind being treated alphabetically."

¶

"Outside of a dog, a book is man's best friend. Inside of a dog, it's too dark to read."
                                                —Groucho Marx

¶

Emerson referred to "the Poetry of the Portfolio"—"the work of persons who wrote for the relief of their own minds, and without thought of publication."

¶

Klimt said that to write anything, even a short note, made him "seasick."

※

Lao-tzu: "The Way that can be spoken of is not the True Way."

※

—X got up on his hind legs and …
—X is filling a much-needed gap
—backbencher; ward-heeler
—*un mutilé de guerre*
—frog-marched

※

optima dies prima fugit

※

Motionless, deep in his mind lies the past the poet's forgotten,
Till some small experience wake it to life and a poem's begotten,
Words its presumptive primordia, Feeling its field of induction,
Meaning its pattern of growth determined during construction.
—WHA, note in "New Year Letter"

※

"Some people think that luxury is the opposite of poverty. Not so. It is the opposite of vulgarity."
—Coco Chanel

※

"Technique in art … has about the same value as technique in lovemaking. That is to say, heartfelt ineptitude has its appeal and so does heartless skill, but what you want is passionate virtuosity."
—John Barth

※

"Drawing is not form, it's the way you see form."
—Degas

¶

"Exuberance is Beauty"
—Blake

¶

To the wounds of his victims, Torquemada applied thistle poultices.

¶

Euclid defined a point as having position but no magnitude.

¶

Roethke had submitted "The Lost Son" to *Horizon*. Sonia Brownell (later Orwell) returned it with this remark: "It seemed to us that your poetry was in a way very American in that it just lacked that inspiration, inevitability or quintessence of writing and feeling that distinguishes good poetry from verse."

¶

"Poets are jails. Works are the convicts who escape."
—Cocteau, diary, March 23, 1953

¶

November 11, 1990: In line with Jane for a movie at MOMA. SM approached, said he'd been at the NYU reading last week and had been struck by my new Bishop poem. Did I remember the Cambridge reading of long ago? he asked. I did. Did I remember talking with Lowell about Bishop? I didn't—but he had been listening in. He overheard me asking Cal what might account for EB's popularity. "All the fags like her" was his answer.

¶

Tom Paulin refers to an Irish word *thrawn* to mean a poetry or language where there's "something a bit difficult, a bit contorted," as in Donne or Hopkins or Browning (or Frost, he adds, and Hardy).

※

For the Greeks, memory was "the waker of longing."

※

Happiness is what I most know in life, but grief is what I best understand of it.

※

Harold Bloom: "My favorite prose sentence by Mr. Ezra Pound is in one of his published letters: 'All the Jew part of the Bible is black evil.' And they ask me to take that seriously as a Western mind."

※

"What constitutes adultery is not the hour which a woman gives her lover, but the night which she afterwards spends with her husband."
—George Sand

※

A British critic described Beverly Sills's voice, later in her career, as "part needle, part thread."

※

—rust-proof
—X has floured his sauce
—the talking classes
—fan de siècle
—a slash of gin

※

The Japanese ideogram for "noise" is the ideogram for "woman" repeated three times.

※

"*All* must have prizes," said the Dodo.

※

Schoenberg's transcription of "The Emperor Waltz" for clarinet, violin, cello and harmonium—an image for *translation* in general?

※

My old college teacher Elias Mengel once showed me his copy of Wallace Stevens' *Collected Poems*, which WS had inscribed: "Dear Elias: When I speak of the poem, or often when I speak of the poem, in this book, I mean not merely a literary form, but the brightest and most harmonious concept, or order, of life; and the references should be read with that in mind."

※

Wilde: "only mediocrities develop."

※

Robert Pinget, on his own writing: "You might call it a kind of automatic writing carried out in a state of total consciousness.... I am now convinced that in a work of art we do not try to conjure up beauty or truth. We only have recourse to them—as to a subterfuge—in order to be able to go on breathing."

※

"I have played with quite a few musicians who weren't so good. But as long as they could hold their instruments correct, and display their willingness to play as best they could, I would look over their shoulders and see Joe Oliver and several other great masters from my home town."
—Louis Armstrong

※

Balanchine: "*Apollo* I look back on as a turning point of my life. In its discipline and restraint, in its sustained oneness of tone and feeling, the score was a revelation. It seemed to tell me that I could dare not to use everything, that I, too, could eliminate."

¶

"The closer the look I take at a word, the greater the distance from which it looks back."
—Karl Kraus

¶

Freud on the surrealists (from the journal of Princess Marie Bonaparte): "They send me all their productions. They think I approve what they write. But it isn't art."

¶

The measure of a poem's "immortality" is the later life it has in other poems. Imitation, appropriation—dismemberment and regeneration—by new poets give the old poem its purchase on life.

¶

Pope, on his *Brutus* (of which an outline and eight lines remain): "Though there is none of it writ as yet, what I look upon as more than half the work is already done, for 'tis all exactly planned."

¶

"A book is never a masterpiece. It becomes one."
—from the Goncourts' journal

¶

—*pompier*
—Boot Hill
—majaism (Levine?)
—X's poems are *objets de vertu*
—X's grasp exceeds his reach
—wings-and-flats

¶

Age is a caricature of the self (or the self's body and features). To make someone look funny—or do I mean merely to make fun of someone?—, make him look older.

❡

Nietzsche held that "refinement of cruelty belongs to the springs of art."

❡

Tu nihil in magno doctus reprehendis Homero?
—Horace

❡

Nabokov, *Look at the Harlequins!* (p. 44): "In those days I seemed to have had two muses: the essential, hysterical, genuine one, who tortured me with elusive snatches of imagery and wrung her hands over my inability to appropriate the magic and madness offered me; and her apprentice, her palette girl and stand-in, a little logician, who stuffed the torn gaps left by her mistress with explanatory or meter-mending fillers which became more and more numerous the further I moved away from the initial, evanescent, savage perfection."

1984

Idea: from the Greek: form, notion, class.

We've forgotten form's abstract. We tend to oppose it to content, which we suppose closer to idea, and in which "in" gets into the act ...

Form affirms, who said that? (Merrill?) Crystals are alive, radiation scares us partly because of half-life (the uncanny, says Freud, isn't the perfectly strange: it's the half-familiar). Science won't let us class things as inert anymore and hallelujah. If everything's alive we better broaden our respects ...

¶

We think "class" the sign of a distinction: a high-mindedness at work. But it's also an exclusion, an ease: it's easier to think of fewer possibilities. But let me not too easily assume the truth is complicated, only, either: nature pulls back from the welter of minutiae and forms a spiral, too.

¶

1985

January 21: There are so many ways to be unwise, not the least of which lies in being too smart, too quick off the block, too full of one's own to listen to anybody else's. The longer I live the less I like glib, can stand to be or hear it ...

¶

March 16: Charleston, Illinois, 1:48 AM. Hearing of Mitchell Toney's nearing death.

And when he had opened the seventh seal, there was silence in heaven about the space of half an hour ...

And I heard a voice from heaven saying unto me, seal up those things which the seven thunders uttered, and write them not.

¶

McHugh

March 25: Jacksonville, Florida:

> Illness is the night-side of life, a more onerous citizenship. Everyone who is born holds dual citizenship, in the kingdom of the well and in the kingdom of the sick. Although we all prefer to use only the good passport, sooner or later each of us is obliged, at least for a spell, to identify ourselves as citizens of that other place ...
> —Susan Sontag

¶

April 14: We live in a forgetfulness, a distraction. All the little irritants, flat tires, hurt fingers, laundry, complaining co-workers, become (or pass) our lives *for us*. And on the dining room table in the house where Mitchell lay (or, less frequently, walked) dying, were spread the annual income tax papers of his parents ...

¶

April 25: Individually we die out and it's not the *moment* of dying that's intolerable, it's the *endlessness* ... No one with a mission or a big hope helps. What helps is humble: a gratuity, not a salary. On the bus, a woman smiles and asks am I all right; in the fast food place a man offers extra coffee; I mean happy is only lucky (I used to say I was lucky and mean for life! Characteristically lucky! But hap *is* chance). Happy is lucky like that, only for a relative second, before the second splits ...

¶

May 18: Air near Denver

To live with a more constant attention to the depths, not just the surfaces of experience. To work without loss of heart. The last words Mitchell said, according to Charles, as Charles was trying to feed him a spoonful of water and trembled while trying, were these: "Keep calm." In the long lovelessness, not to disdain the ordinary, ever. Not to get suckered back into shallow businesses ... old fears and vanities seem petty ... have I a greater capacity for courage now? greater motivation for it? This all sounds trite to me. It's for poems to save such ferocities of feeling from death by commonplace. It's for poetry to shake the saying ...

※

May 24: All this homilizing and resolve of mine sicken me. Most of the time I just feel sore, I haul around the animal of my shot passions. It hurts to breathe ...

What women call a period is really a semi-colon, meaning more to come ... Blood out of men, all at once, might be a period.

※

May 14: 1st dream: letter from the dead: "No love, no words, no apples, no oranges. No pairs."

※

May 22: 2nd dream: Mitchell, sick, asks me to reach into the top shelf of a closet for gifts he wants to give people. Each gift has a name. I'm supposed to deliver them. When I've gotten the last one down I am disappointed to notice it isn't for me. Then I realize what my gift is: I'm the giver.

※

July 6: (in the air, en route from Boston to North Carolina)
Life can be awful for children, I think—the containments must seem endless. As we get older, we contain *ourselves*, invoke ends to make unpleasant presents *pass*able ... This doesn't prepare us well for death, this comfort-by-living-in-the-future. In planes I think most often of death, and my dead friends—the perspective is so out-of-this-world ...

※

July 7: My waking life is still a constant attempt at dialogue with Mitchell. I'd talk to mediums, scryers, crazies, priests, or mynah birds if they said they could talk with the dead. Every dark, every sky, every altitude is his dark, his sky, his altitude.

It's no consolation to be told he survives in our memories, or in his work. It's his experience I can't stop wondering about, mourning after; one feels so close to someone—how can they just GO OUT, as a fire goes out? Surely it's *my* incapacity that separates us. I can't believe life's complication could come to so obliterating a simplicity. We can't live in ourselves alone.

I share St. Augustine's regret at "selling the art of words" to pay off debts (he's speaking of teaching rhetoric, of course) ... In two years I hope I'm done with universities. It is monastic life I half-crave, with its studies, solitudes, illuminated texts (and well-bred—never sour—grapes) ...

I visited Mitchell's home town, Jacksonville. Rented a car and spent some time at the beach, a stretch of throbbing vacancy edged by foam, littered by the come-and-gone, and lettered by commercial biplane ("How about an ice-cold Busch?"). At dusk one particular mile of boardwalk was purpled and hearted, pumping music, cruised by families, lovers, jacks and jills, dancers, desirers—I was almost the only white one there. I liked that neighborhood of urgencies and tones ...

But the grave was a bald spot in the grass. Florida grass isn't much to write home about anyway; the grave is marked with no stone yet, and in dead sun ... I wish I could plant trees, roses, a whole fucking Eden where he is.

¶

July 15: Mitchell's mom and dad got up at 6 AM to see me off at the airport. His father's horoscope this morning read: "It may seem the events since early May were designed to test your spirit. Now it will become apparent you've been freed from a narrower way of life." The early morning in Florida is clear and warm and dewy, with a pink cast on water and leaves.

If anything could turn me into a Christian churchgoer it would be black gospel music. When that music comes on I can't stay still, my liveliness leaps, I actually feel great joy and great capacity for tears. Deeper, farther back than any other music in me goes that one: I came from it, I'm headed for it …

¶

July 27: Home in Maine, I think of Mitchell and of death daily, half the time in wonder. There's a blessing (the French word blesser means to wound) in it but I miss the man; I miss men. But I love Eastport, my niche; it's my grounding and joy. And even that will be lost, huh, God, old buddy, old pal? The water's beautiful, also the islands, proportions, clouds (which are air-islands, matched to their partners in the Passamaquoddy Bay below), boats. I'm drinking bad Chablis on the Cannery Wharf, where the ferry (a funny tug-and-scow affair) comes and goes each hour. It's bright blue and white and breezy and the big gulls are healthy and clean. But every moment of every day I am sad for the dead.

In general, I crave to share my lucks and passions with someone, but want to let things take their course: half the forces I ever exerted (of personality, will, wish) finally seemed unwise. And now I may not flirt or wave at death, with any flag or flourish, red or white. A long unease and then a real disease, that's the prospectus. At the bottom of this cup is embossed "Sweetheart Plastics." "Red!," said Mitchell, "Where do you get your reputation? (You leap from lips to leaves in fall. Not until we leave do you stay …) What do you mean in cemeteries where, plastic, you last?"

¶

November 19: Is happiness in life by chance *mal*adaptive? I wonder. Is death a moment or an enormity? (I can't prepare for it with my old addictive joy in futures. Or is that just what I'm doing? Constructing a plausible form of future to digest?) When I'm happy I look forward. I forget death. Is this then poor happiness or poor understanding of death? Or do we need both, the love and the relinquishment of futures, each in its time?

McHugh

The main trouble in my life is this struggle with death. My almost constant attention to it—my reluctance to approve its purest democracy: utter arbitrariness in time. Since Mitchell died I can't rest without coming to some peace about this (i.e. I cannot rest). Perhaps rest will finally mean letting it go—I keep examining my own willingness to die (I need an electron microscope to see it).

The work of my life has been to live well (but what 'well' means has changed—not to distinguish myself anymore, now it must be to be *with* and *like* others, even—this change of emphasis is surely salutary). Last night reading something incidental I fell into such a weeping *it wept me;* I couldn't keep reading. I went to bed with no hope in my spirit, only a sense of the common horror, what we spend our lives ignoring but are headed for—our only outcome ...

I do think time is my big blindness—it's such an unacknowledged tyrant, its arbitrariness so man-made, its terms so universally assumed (I remember how I resisted learning to tell time as a child—it went against my grain, and took forever [!] to swallow)—once you enter that world, as though you'd entered the world of language, you leave all other worlds behind, you actually *contract* (engage *and* diminish) experience to match it.

So now may death free us to the unspeakable not only in its social/local/vernacular sense (as horror) but also to the unspeakability which, simply, preceded language—to the unspeakable which is too great to be shrunk into any one human language—(unspeakability that could yet become a tribute!). Unspeakable understanding as greatened understanding, not amputated, in an instant adding another dimension (not just the two- or three-D axes we imagine, but a depth freed of our characteristic biological speeds). Timelessness in that second we thought the last ...

¶

Book title: *Done For* (generates nice readings but nasty reviews, too tempting for bilious critics).

¶

Translation tip for Bulgarians visiting America: Whenever anyone on TV (except a whore or hotelier) says "Take care of them," he means "Kill them."

¶

1988

March 15: "Him you do not teach to fly, teach to fall faster."
—Nietzsche

¶

August 8: My lilac, lilies and potentilla are all spreading! Two years ago, they started as little snippets, rootlets, really, at my hand; but now their own nature takes over and they spread ... Last month I dreamt there was no self, except in the faint sense of a presiding uneasiness; otherwise all was otherwise; no selfwise existed. This effect was quite literal in the dream. Like a great deal of my dreaming since 1985, this was more of an illumination than a narrative. It was a sense, an experience, I never had awake.

Awake, nevertheless, I'm in a peaceful niche of life, here at home in Maine, with bright flags of kitchen towels on the line (my prayer flags) and the yardwork showing fruits (at last this year 4 small pears on one of the trees).

¶

1989

October 29: Syracuse, NY
In my solitude again (these semesters away from home are getting harder) I'm grateful for Chekhov's journals and Kafka's diaries. They are oddly contrary to expectation: in the former, a swift and lacerating outline of character ("She had too little skin to cover her face: in order to open her eyes she had to close her mouth, and vice versa"); full of moral over- and under-toning; while in the latter (Kafka) the most prominent feature (after the constant self-denigration and complaint)

is the glimpses or snippets of people *seen*—utterly free from moral coloration—"young little girl, 18 years old; nose, shape of head, blonde, seen fleetingly in profile; came out of the church"; or, "the dirty little barefoot girl running along in her shift with her hair blowing," or "5-year-old girl; orchard, little path to the main alley; hair, nose, shining grandchild," or "old father and his elderly daughter. He reasonable, slightly stooped, with a pointed beard, a little cane held behind his back. She broadnosed, with a strong lower jaw, round distended face; turned clumsily on her broad hips." My gratitude to the former is for the quality of his judgment, and to the latter for the quality of his freedom from it (not at all what I'd expected from their respective fictions). Those glimpses of Kafka's, so spare and structural, like sketches for a painting, but always poised in three or four dimensions (of which time is more obsessive than the other three), particularly astonished me. Glimpses of strangers, saved as gestures, turns of head—people through a window or a door (Kafka's window or door!) A glimmer arises for me of that sense of "realization" I study and crave and so seldom can actually feel flame up in my life—the deepest understanding that ANOTHER PERSON LIVED, I mean so lived as I do, the feeling so deep it's free of tense—we fail *to believe in* ("realize") those around us *in the present* as absolutely as we do anyone in history. So when I say these glimpses turn now and then to realization in me, the equivalent is out of time: "this person *is* alive" (not only "this person *was* alive"); and even "I *am* alive" (a sentence in which every word means the same thing). This last realization, the sudden shuddering understanding "I am alive" is so foregone we leave it till the last: it is achieved better the nearer we are to death. "I am alive" can most honestly be said when it's about to be untrue.

Yet the presence I am groping to characterize amounts to a *solidarity* with all other human experience, and not an *exile* from it. In my solitude I come closer to human being than I ever can in close-ups and absorptions—(am I excusing myself? comforts of abstraction? Never actually helping the sick child through the night ... Not that I don't have the instinct: I don't have the occasion).

But I must more precisely imagine what IS: the sick I *don't* see, they exist. And must need help. Do I not hear them? I hear clearly the call of the dying, but I haven't gone to their side. Instead I sit somewhere with manuscripts and drink coffee and consult with those paged sensibilities (read the dead). How much good could I do?, the shirker asks; every act excludes more than it includes (is this true? not if infinities are nested everywhere! What's *more*, then?—or as William Bronk puts it, "What would more *mean*?") And how could "good" have a "much" before it? The debate must keep arising in me out of a sense of wasted life: my sense of selfishness—powers bounded by material safekeepings. Shall I someday have the courage of my yearnings? to rid myself of job, pride, houses, decades of attachment? Decade, decadence. What's of moment? (Be born now, not *then*.)

Jane Miller

1984–1990

"... a moment of truth. Someone closes his eyes for a few seconds. When he opens them again he sees that nothing has changed down the street outside his window. He gives a start."
—"Terror of the Outlaws," Wim Wender

¶

honeycomb: "A structure of 6-sided cells constructed from beeswax by honeybees to hold honey and eggs." Verb: riddle, to fill with holes

¶

"The man who can resist humiliation can quickly forget it; but the man who can long tolerate it must long remember it."
—Vaclav Havel, *Living in Truth*

¶

Caliente

So I shut off the light and listened to the rain.
It finally cooled things down.
I'd swum,
& gotten something to eat,
couscous, a carrot, & then settled in,
naked, early,
& had nothing to do so
turned on the radio,
an ordinary lyrical solo,
& on
into evening, gratifying,
lonely, the steady
downpour broken with thunder,
lightning stumbling
& limbs crisscrossing the sky
now pearl,
willow, cherry & aspen
heavy, a credible
time to remember other rain,
but I did not for more

than a moment test myself
against your favorite season
breaking seamlessly in,
& only a little dreamt your skin
characteristically floating on mine
(forgive me a memory of coastal Spain,
misty red grapes—).

※

vegetarian dream: with mother: going to buy meat. get to butcher's house where, in front of me, animals are cut open alive. length-wise from underneath. one walks off, presumably to die alone, and the pain of that moment makes me never want to eat meat again.

※

gazpacho blend: 1 medium-sized garlic clove, crushed
        1 whole green pepper
        1 tablesp white vinegar
        1 tablesp olive oil
        1 whole cucumber
        6 large ripe tomatoes
        thinly sliced, a third of a white onion
        tiny piece of day-old bread
        1/4 cup water
        pepper to taste
                        —from Pedro Almodovar

※

John Cage, on art: "It must have to do with our placement of attention. I'm trying to speak now or think now without regard to intention or non-intention ... I work with questions whereas many people work with choices."

Cage words from Harvard lectures: Method Structure Intention Disciple Notation Indeterminancy Interpenetration Imitation Devotion Circumstances Variable structure Nonunderstanding Contingency Inconsistency Performance

Miller

Course idea: use Cage words parallel to student portfolios each week of semester —discuss their work next to his word.

Cage: "Art is an imitation of nature, not as she is but in her manner of operation."

Cage: "What I wanted to give up was control, whether it's random to one extent or another is not a concern of mine."

¶

That's not a life, that's a dance floor, and those aren't lips, you asshole, that's lipstick.

¶

Seminar idea: Imagination and politics:
> Terrence des Pres, *Praises and Dispraises*
> Kenneth Burke, *The Philosophy of Literary Form*
> Charles Simic, *The Uncertain Certainty*
> Heidegger, *Poetry, Language, Thought*
> Wallace Stevens, *The Necessary Angel*
> Eliot, *On Poetry and Poets*
> Cavafy, *Collected Poems*

¶

"Did not the Goncourts write that the artists of the great age of Japanese art changed names many times in their careers? I like that: they wanted to safeguard their freedom."

—Henri Matisse, *Jazz*

¶

"The poet gives his [sic] whole life such a voluntary steep incline that it is impossible for it to exist in the vertical line of biography where we expect to meet it."

—Boris Pasternak, *Safe Conduct*

¶

After reading my first two books on an evening when I intended to start a poem toward a new book, it pleased me to have suffused the work with a heady climate, lots of people, food, places, times, bright glare—not bad, since so much is missing. Poems dressed in deep reds, ochres, they warrant some affection, they can't help themselves, girls at a beach, all legs, close to the water, to earth, in a kind of motion; one is especially young.

¶

irises
strawberries
canteloupe
shrimp
crab
ginger
garlic
olive oil
red lettuce
watercress
red cabbage

umbelliferous, airy-flowered herbs: dill, fennel, caraway

medicinal plants affecting the brain, nervous system, speech, shoulders, arms: lavender, marjoram, gotu kola, parsnips, …

¶

"This afternoon in Lima it's raining. And I remember
the cruel caverns of my ingratitude;
my block of ice laid on her poppy,
stronger than her crying, 'Don't be this way!'"
                                    —Vallejo, "Down to the Dregs"

¶

sweat, tears, piss, and come, marigolds, dahlias, hyacinth, white lilac

Miller

Sex: everyone wants to know how others do it: come for me

¶

the speed of night riders
read the directions carefully

hey—get started already!

is it conversational or can you
deliver meaning

not a compliment, a remark

not an attack, a regard, not a demand,
a voice, not a _____.

away, from what?

a fake logos, naturally
I'll let you throw your coat down

¶

Back in the hotel, fairly uneventful, except I'm really hungry—have to sleep it off. Very quiet, as it turns out. Band gone, people gone. I don't know, I somehow end up in a hotel room by the sea thousands of miles from family and friends. I don't have to keep doing this, but I do.

¶

When they met by accident in the airport, each coming from a different place and going, for a brief time anyway, to the same small town, they were both tired, had nothing to say. Their lives were diverging, already had. Was it too late? It would seem so. But then, reality never interested them in the least. It would be wrong. Always.

¶

"The wheat is high enough for you to lose your dog in. It is tawny like an animal, but tinged with green and around the skin of its ears with violet."

—John Berger, along the eastern side of the main train to Moscow

❡

"There are so many things between lovers of which only they can judge."

—George Sand

❡

"When I have arranged a bouquet for the purpose of painting it, I always turn to the side I did not plan."

—Matisse, *Jazz*

❡

"Freedom, real freedom, not just talk about it, freedom, dropped out of the sky, freedom beyond our expectations, freedom by accident, through a misunderstanding."

—Pasternak

❡

A rose of crinolines on fire

❡

"The states of the soul are inscribed in the landscape."

—Primo Levi, *Other People's Trades*

❡

"Once in one's lifetime one ought to walk so far that one loses all the skin off one's feet and really begins to speak to oneself. Otherwise it happens only in dreams."

—Max Frisch, *Montaux*

Robert Morgan

1970

Poetry exists in the speech of the nonindustrialized people around us, and to a smaller degree in all speech. But you must know what to listen for to find it.

¶

1971

Failure makes you aware of the death growing in your flesh. But at the very instant of pain we see everything clearly, as in the illumination of lightning's brief maps. Yet, whatever the failure, at some point you find you can go on; things open up again, the oxygen is still there.

¶

1976

We are a continent discovered by going West to reach the sacred, legendary East, suggesting perhaps that our best motions are backwards, countermotions, the tacking done by reverse English, so to speak. Every good poem is a kind of declaration of independence, a fusing of ideal and literal. Our reaction to old England forks with the gothic inwardness of Poe and the expansive idealism of Emerson.

¶

In our century we have often hoped for the primitive and mythic, only to reveal our decadence. What spiritual carnality we aspire to, only to find carnality. Through our vernacularity we hope to discuss the subtle and elevated, make unity of the clutter, raise the jargon of science to a sacred language, and end too often with abstraction, flatness.

¶

Our most common modern form is autobiography, confession, self-analysis, allied to the peculiar narcissism of so much contemporary art. The danger is that with no audience, and no hope of an audience, poets will write only to themselves. My horror is of much action and little originality. Better creative indolence.

¶

Language is by its very nature affirmative, because the act of articulating, even anger, violent emotion, is controlled response. Suicide prevention agencies know that talk is the first step toward will and work. The elemental sentence is the forwarding of energy from one point of being to another. Language is in a literal sense constructive, requires an act of making. It is at once constructive and destructive, as is perception itself. Language is the shaping of breath, implying deeper syntax beyond speech. Language is the understructure of the collective imagination.

¶

Poetry moves both in and out of time as it occupies space and rears back toward original form. The two motions are functions of each other, and the distance between them is the thickness and depth of the poem. The music of poetry derives more from economy, quickness, accuracy, than from meter or even the natural rhythm of the sentences. The mere music of language is rather dull. But the spare sentence muscled with substance resounds, and cools gravity.

¶

A poem with long lines reads faster than a poem with short lines because the line, like a pendulum swing, tends to have the same duration no matter how many words it contains.

¶

Nothing works in poetry better than narrative, or at least the hint of narrative. It lights up even ordinary images and phrasing. Get the tension by story, get the attention by tension. Something must be happening in poetry as in fiction. The very nature of language is narrative, the relation of something going on, subject, verb, object.

¶

Morgan

But poetry moves and delights us in short passages, almost never in whole poems, at least almost never in poems of any length. It is those sparks of detail and music that we remember and return to. And the sense of wholeness and authority implied by the fragments.

※

Poetry is elision, a leaving out. I don't want to be a sharecropper with the harvest I take from the soil. I would rather give all away. I want word-telescopes, not hairshirts of wisdom. I go for mythic realism, real icons. A poem must witness the collison of two or more ideas to generate energy. The shape of the conflict can be formal (fencing) or freestyle (wrestling).

※

I do not believe in deifying the imagination. Such stress on process seems technical and limited. I prefer haecceity as much as symmetry, and don't want to starve the vulgar life-giving faculties by worshipping imagination. Poetry seems to be written best on the brink of chaos, where it draws from turbulence but is free enough to cool into form.

※

1978

As Chaucer in his time bypassed the deadend of the nominalist/realist controversy that dominated Oxford and Paris by simply ignoring it and telling stories, so today we must overlook the fussiness of contemporary intellectualism. We must feel the authority and faith in the power of language to delight and inform, and not exhaust ourselves with trivial linguistic hairsplitting.

※

Poetry is always a turning, and a turning back. Trope, figure. Never a proceeding in the logical and programmatic, never an agenda. Poetry is the verso, the reverse side of any image, the surprise reversal. Poetry does not argue, it discovers and affirms. It begins with the nondenominated fact and names the unnameable. Look to the least poetic subject for paydirt, and to the least poetic language.

¶

I like poems in fragments, things with rough and sharp edges that sometimes cut unexpectedly, that cannot be handled too easily and always with safety. One piece of broken quartz can shave an ax handle, same as an expensive plane. Lines are pieces of the shattered original diamond.

¶

Mind generates language to prove it will never die.

¶

An image is a language tensor, the compact union of two separate systems of reference. The pharaoh's dream of riding in a crystal.

¶

I would take the filth and stinky cans and sawdust bags, soot and broken bulbs, and crush the mess into a compact ingot, into a fleshy diamond.

¶

One acre will eat a family.

¶

The fictional integrity of a poem should not be violated by mouthing about its composition. If we are reading a text we know it is text, not actual experience.

¶

It's the gap in the circuit that makes the welding fire, that cuts the hardest steel, and joins seamlessly.

¶

It is the time just before discovery that we look back on with such feeling, such nostalgia, creating now the missed expectancy.

¶

Morgan

The present grows on the rubbish and unfinished business of the past. Decadence makes the richest soil. Our times are well manured.

¶

Poetry awakens what is most other and yet most ourselves.

¶

1991

I wonder about the influence of TV commercials on poetics. Nothing in our culture is so finely honed, so elegantly compressed. Children go around quoting commercials the way children of former times chanted nursery rhymes. At a cost of many thousands of dollars per second, commercials have to do their work quickly, through the surprising image, the implicit narrative of romance, aspiration. And they must stick in the memory. They suggest the vivid fragment which is the model of so much contemporary poetry. And yet the commercial is completely without depth, without the reach of poetry.

¶

It is not the "chaos" of contemporary life which is so notable, but rather the predictability, the routines. Our lives are organized down to the second, our days and weeks and years planned to the hour. In spite of all the talk of uncertainty and loss of belief, people are perhaps surer of who they are and where they fit in creation than ever before, thanks to science and psychoanalysis. It may indeed be the mystery of existence they miss most, a world haunted by forces beyond their understanding.

¶

Could the randomness, the rubato, the very freedom of free verse, be a rebellion against the tidiness of so much contemporary life? In truly chaotic times, in a world of threat and catastrophic change, the predictability of regular versification would be welcomed, as a way of containing, and seeming to control, the welter of experience, the colliding systems of understanding.

In any case, it is no excuse for poetry that it merely mirrors the confusion of its times. A landfill would serve as well. As it is no excuse for obscure poetry that it can be explained. One danger of the academic environment has always been that it values the gloss over the poem. The primary business of poetry is delight, complex delight and praise, whether hex or haecceity.

¶

The ruled space of a great poem is a kind of periodic chart, implying in compact symbols a whole universe, animated, elusive, changing, even while arranged in lattices permanent as crystal. As all history is implicit in language, so all matter is implicit in each element, and all voices in each vowel. Each branch speaks a dialect of water, but evokes the ocean.

¶

Look at a poem written a decade ago, the page yellowed and covered with dust. Does a line shine through, a single word? Does a thought there live beyond the writer's enthusiasm in the act of making? Is there exhilaration of the intersection of time and eternity? When the dust is brushed away, what breathes, what demands to be spoken again?

Lisel Mueller

April 18–July 15, 1991

Marie Luise Kaschnitz wrote that it might be instructive for a poet to examine her work and make a list of words she has favored, as a way of finding out about her preoccupations. In her own case, she found to her surprise that her imagery is dense with chestnut and plane trees, but not conifers; that she favors clouds but not stars; that wind and water are ubiquitous, but snow almost absent; that certain flowers keep recurring; that birds always show up in migratory flocks. Of course she soon gave up; the game became boring. I wonder what such a dictionary would tell us about ourselves, and whether it would lead us back to childhood.

¶

The beginning of a poem by a child in a pediatric hospital, where long-term patients are encouraged to write:

> I was born between God
> and Jesus.
> My father was a heart,
> my mother was a bow and arrow.

¶

Found poem:

> What place is there for the soul to go after death?
> In heaven there's no more room between the stars.
> Who builds the houses of the angels?

(Translated excerpts from a German review of *Heaven: A History* by Colleen McDonnell and Bernhard Lang.)

In "Lucifer in Starlight" George Meredith calls the stars "the brain of Heaven."

¶

In response to criticism that his fiction was negative and pessimistic, Max Frisch replied that it was much more negative not to suffer by not presenting negative things, because if you suffer it means you want something else, something more, out of life. Praising things as they are is just giving in.

Speaking of painters who understand tragedy, Michael Brenson of *The New York Times* said something similar. He said that if they did not understand tragedy they would not understand hope.

※

A friend tells me that lately he finds it hard to write poetry. In order to write poetry he has to love the world, he says, and the world has become so unlovable.

Yes, the world has become extraordinarily violent, corrupt, cruel and shallow. When societies divide into people who despair and people who couldn't care less, and the power in the hands of the last group keeps growing—in the United States as well—anger is easier to come by than love. How to do it, how to turn anger against brutality and injustice into great poetry; how to burn like Blake, like Yeats in "The Second Coming?" How to deal with the suffering of others in a genre that has traditionally been a projection of the self? And how can we be presumptuous enough to identify ourselves with victims of horrors we are sheltered from?

※

> Who am I to speak for the homeless,
> I have a house to live in;
> who am I to speak for beaten women,
> I am not one of them
>
> What right have I to raise my voice
> like an angel proclaiming the gospel;
> who am I to palm off my poems
> as loaves and fishes
>
> What right have I to say *my life*
> as if it were singular,
> as if it could be distinguished
> from the life cycle of my species
>
> How can I praise the light
> as if I had no need for darkness;

> how can I speak of darkness
> and keep still about what is done there
>
> What good is my safehouse of words
> to the millions of people dying
> on the roofless roads of our century;
> who am I to speak for them
>
> What can I say about courage
> when my back has not been to the wall;
> how can I speak in the name
> of anyone but myself
>
> when I know that is not enough

¶

Still, love *is* the impulse from which poetry springs. Even dark poems. Especially dark poems. To know the worst and write in spite of that, that must be love. To celebrate what's on the other side of the darkness. Truly great poetry has always sprung from love-in-spite-of, like love for a deeply flawed person.

And if it's true, as Williams wrote, that people die from the lack of what is found in poems, then poetry must not be trivial, peripheral, ivory-towerish, as it is often accused of being; then we have a responsibility to speak to and for others. Certainly that means acknowledging suffering. But it also means to heal, to bring delight and hope. It implies consolation. How to console without being false, shallow or sentimental: I find that the hardest challenge.

¶

Yehudi Amichai demands that every poem should be the last poem, written as if it contained the last thing the poet would ever say, shaped to contain a condensation of all the messages of his or her life. It should be a virtual will.

¶

Note on language: Our everyday speech is so suffused with metaphor that we can hardly say three consecutive sentences without using it, never mind the fact that it is overwhelmingly "dead" metaphor, i.e., no longer felt as such. Not by a native speaker anyway. But for a foreigner, even though he has absorbed dictionary, grammar book English, it can be a living hurdle. I am imagining a conversation between two businessmen, one American and one a foreigner. At one point in the conversation the American leans back and says, "The ball is in your court." The other man looks bewildered. "It's your turn," the American explains. The foreigner turns around. "No, I mean it's up to you." Up? Why up? He casts his eyes toward the ceiling. The American tries once more. "It means it's your move. Like in chess." Ah. His visitor's eyes light up. He knows chess. He understands. But what about the ball?

¶

"It speaks to me," we say about something that touches us in a special way. Language, communication; Martin Buber's I-Thou relationship operating even when one of the two is a speechless object.

¶

H. writes to me about the sad state of her 93-year-old bedridden mother, a stroke victim. "There's only one thing to wish for, but of course one must not say it," she writes. As if words were still magic, and—though she wants to spare her mother further meaningless life—she does not dare be the agent of her death.

¶

When I give a reading I sometimes read "Late Hours," a poem from my recent book, which refers in part to my husband and me reading Chekhov's short stories together, and whose last lines are

>What luxury, to be so happy
>that we can grieve
>over imaginary lives.

I like to read the poem because I feel these lines so strongly, am so aware of the (undeserved) luxury of happiness. I've never had a direct response to them from a listener and don't know how audiences feel about them. But recently I've had a response from a reviewer living in Tel Aviv.

She quoted the lines and added her comment: "A luxury poets cannot afford!" So I am directed back toward the real sorrows of the real world.

❡

Note on language: I wonder how much the meaning of a word influences our attitude toward the object it denotes. Since German was my first language, I grew up with the name "Flügel" for grand piano, so that instrument is for me a dark, shiny wing, not necessarily grand, but capable of soaring, bearing music upward and outward, releasing it to air and freedom. And even now I can't think of the mullein as an unglamorous, oversized weed, since in my childhood language this proudly erect plant is called "Königskerze," a king's candle, and I grew up with a notion of its dignity. I've learned to my satisfaction that there are more respectful common names for it in English too, such as Jacob's staff and Aaron's rod.

❡

Nostalgia doesn't do any good, but old people have always indulged in it. What is new is that even the young are nostalgic these days. People under 30 write novels and poetry collections and memoirs about their childhoods. Never have we been so aware of the fleeting moment. Writers take notes, artists sketch, videotapes roll, each recording the blip of the present, more of a blip all the time.

❡

"Poetry is in love with the instant and seeks to relive it in the poem, thus separating it from sequential time and turning it into a fixed present."
—Octavio Paz

A poem is
to keep a now
for then.
—Felix Pollak

❡

Outside the house language keeps changing. Now that it's August cicadas decide it is their time; they fill our ears all night. The birds are no longer raucous; mostly they twitter like old ladies, though the catbird continues its impeccable imitation and the crows are irrepressible. The bullfrogs in the little lakes next door are gone; we miss their cow-like moos. The bees hum discreetly, and the flies, newborns this month, are beginning their black buzzing. The trees are a long way from rattling yet; still heavy with summer they offer us the language of silence.

Mary Oliver

Who would tell the mockingbird his song is frivolous, since it lacks words?

❡

Do you think the wren ever dreams of a better house?

❡

Though you have not seen them, there are swans, even now
tapping from the egg and emerging
into the sunlight.
They know who they are.

❡

When will you have a little pity for
every soft thing
that walks through the world,
yourself included?

❡

When the main characters of one's life die, is there any replacement?
Or, is there anything *but* replacement?

❡

I hope I don't live to be a hundred/
in the arms of my family.

❡

When you first saw her—beauty, the dream—the human vortex of your life—or him—did you stop, and stand in the crisp air, breathing like a tree? Did you change your life?

❡

The small deadly voice
of vanity.

❡

It's better for the heart to break/
than not to break.

❡

All my life, and it has not come to any more than this:
beauty and terror.

❡

Something totally unexpected,
like a barking cat.

❡

Sharpsburg: "One well-read member of the 9th New York wrote long afterward: The mental strain was so great that I saw at that moment the singular effect mentioned, I think, in the life of Goethe on a similar occasion—the whole landscape for an instant turned slightly red."
—B. Caton, *Mr. Lincoln's Army*

❡

The sword, after all, is not built just to glitter like a ribbon in the air.

❡

But I want to say something more uncomfortable even than that.

❡

"And then, who knows? Perhaps we will be taken in hand by certain memories, as if by angels."
—M. Yourcenar

❡

Molasses, an orange, fennel seed, anise seed, rye flour, two cakes of yeast.

❡

Oliver

Culture: power, money and security (therefore).
Art: hope, vision, the soul's need to speak.

¶

All culture developed as some wild, raw creature strived to live better and longer.

¶

Dreams don't have time/space constriction. Of course, in a way, Adam naming the things of this world was narrowing his horizons. Perhaps dreaming is meditating, before language existed. Animals certainly dream.

¶

Language, the tool of consciousness.

¶

The line is the device upon which the poem spins itself into being. Verse, versus, *vers*, turn the plough, turn the line. It is impossible to measure the frustration I feel when, after making careful decisions about where the line should turn, an editor snaps off the long limbs to fit some magazine's column-girth or print-line. Most especially in those instances when it seems so inexplicable—when the criminal act is accomplished not by an editor but by a poet/editor. To make a fuss to a friend is so painful. But I will fuss and fuss, and keep the little leaping goat in his wide pasture.

¶

F. has been to visit us, and now he is gone. The power of last resort, is the power to disrupt.

¶

M. arranging the curtains in the next room. "Hello there, darling moon," I hear her say.

¶

Oliver

If you kill for knowledge, what is the name of what you have lost?

¶

The danger of people becoming infatuated with knowledge. Thoreau gassing the moth to get a perfect specimen. Audubon thrusting the needle into the bittern's heart.

¶

I took the fox bones back into the dunes and buried them. I don't want to hold on to such things anymore. I mean, I'm certainly full of admiration, and curiosity. But I think something else—a reverence that disavows keeping things—must come to us all, sooner or later. Like a gift, an understanding, a more happy excitement than possession. Or, of a sudden—too late!—like a stone between the eyes.

¶

Everybody has to have their little tooth of power. Everybody wants to be able to bite.

¶

About poems that don't work—who wants to see a bird almost fly?

¶

Fairy tales—the great difference is between doing something, and doing nothing.

¶

After a cruel childhood, one must reinvent oneself. Then reimagine the world.

¶

van Gogh—he considered everything, and still went crazy with rapture.

¶

Oliver

A snapping turtle was floating today on Little Sister Pond. Golden Eyes still on Great Pond.

¶

Laughing Gulls fly by the house laughing.
Maybe a hundred pilot whales off the point.

¶

Another collection of women's poetry. The editor in her introduction: "Only one poet I approached refused to be in a women's anthology." Guess who! I wish she had given my name.

¶

All July and into August, Luke and I see foxes. An adult fox with a young pup. The adult serious and nervous and quick. The young one trailing behind, not serious. It reached up, swatted the pine boughs with a black paw before it vanished under the trees.

¶

Hundreds of gannets feeding just offshore, plunging, tufts of water rising with a white up-kick. Scary birds, long wings, very white, fearful looking beaks. We opened the car windows and there was no sound but the sound of their wings rustling. They fed at three or four places, then were gone much farther out. We were at the right place at the right time.

¶

"I am doing pretty well, gathering energy, working ... and every now and then *timor mortis* descends over me like midnight."

Letter from D.H.

¶

D.B., reviewing *House of Light,* complains of the people in my poems—"the likes of van Gogh, Buddha, Michelangelo, Jesus, Blake, Mahler," a "company of the misunderstood, the martyred ..." he says. Dear Lord,

Oliver

imagine classifying these people, these iridescent people, as misunderstood and martyred!

¶

He also suggests that not many can afford the "luxury of expansive natural isolation." Living as I do, I presume he means, though I wonder what he knows about it. Well, I will consider his remark while I walk downbeach to see if I can find some clams or sea rocket for tonight's dinner. Otherwise, it's van Gogh potatoes again.

¶

Just at the lacy edge of the sea, a dolphin's skull. Recent, but perfectly clean. And entirely beautiful. I held it in my hands, I was so excited I was breathless. What will I do?

¶

Three deer near the path to Oak Head—of course now they always make me think of Luke. Happiness by association.

¶

Who knows, maybe the root is the flower/
of that other life.

¶

Lee, as he was dying, called out, "Strike the tent!" Stonewall Jackson said at the end, softly as I imagine it, "Let us cross over the river and rest under the shade of the trees."

¶

The translation of experience into contemplation, and the placement of this contemplation within the formality of a certain kind of language, with no intent to make contact—be it across whatever thin or wild a thread—with the spiritual condition of the reader, is not poetry. Archibald MacLeish: Here is the writer, and over there—there is "the mystery of the universe." The poem exists—indeed, gets itself written,

Oliver

in the relation *between* the man and the world. The three ingredients of poetry: the mystery of the universe, the aura of spiritual curiosity, the energy of language.

And what is the universe, as far as we are concerned? Leo Frobenius: "It was first the animal world, in its various species, that impressed mankind as a mystery, and that, in its character of admired immediate neighbor, evoked the impulse to imitative identification. Next, it was the vegetable world and the miracle of the fruitful earth, wherein death is changed into life. And finally the focus of attention lifted to the mathematics" of the heavens.

Art cannot separate from these first examples which willed it into existence. Say such forces belong now only to dream or nightmare or to Jung's (our) collective unconscious—or to the ecologically sensitive—I say it's entirely more primal than that. Poetry was born in the relationship between men of earth and the earth itself. Without perceptual experience of life on this earth, how could the following lines be meaningful?

"It is the east, and Juliet is the sun."   Or,

"And what rough beast, its hour come round at last,
Slouches toward Bethlehem to be born?"

I think as an ecologist. But I feel as a member of a great family—one that includes the elephant and the wheat stalk as well as the school teacher and the industrialist. This is not a mental condition, but a spiritual condition. Poetry is a product of our history, and our history is inseparable from the natural world. Now, of course, in the hives and dungeons of the cities, poetry cannot console, it carries no weight, for the pact between the natural world and the individual has been broken. There is no more working for harvest—only hunting, for profit. Lives are no longer exercises in pleasure and valor, but only the means to the amassment of worldly goods. If poetry is ever to become meaningful to such persons, *they* must take the first step—away from their materially bound and self-interested lives, toward the trees, and the waterfall. It is not poetry's fault that it has so small an audience, so little effect upon

Oliver

the frightened, money-loving world. Poetry, after all, is not a miracle. It is an effort to formalize (ritualize) individual moments and the transcending effects of these moments into a music that all can use. It is the song of our species.

¶

It's almost 6 a.m. The mockingbird is still singing. I'm on my way to the ocean, with the sun, just rising, on my left shoulder, and the moon, like a circle of pale snow, lingering on my right.

Gregory Orr

1970

September 21: "Grows smaller"—I love the delicate paradox of that expression. For me, it embodies the absurdity of the static world, the world in which objects are related in an inflexible proportionate way to each other.

❡

September 25: A dream fragment: unloading a truckful of books at a dock parking area to be loaded aboard a huge ship. One of the books a book of Kandinsky's, illustrated. A girl looking at it, just the captions. I telling her the writing/thought is freaky. In the picture she is looking at there is something about "The hand is a carrot, then it is a rabbit; then you go out in the world and see it is both" or "First the hand is a rabbit, then it is a hand again; then you go out in the world/the daylight and see that it is indeed a rabbit."

❡

October 2: My poems sometimes give the illusion of nakedness, but it is a safe nakedness, like undressing in your own room alone. It is not walking naked in a world of people and objects, that would be the true nakedness. My poems are all about the self. My life is all about the self. I can let it in, but I can't let it out. I can receive, but I can't really give.

Naked hour, when suddenly she is no longer there and you can see your mistake: to have thought you could swallow her the way you swallowed the objects of the world and once they had passed through the walls of your body, to set them up in your dark inner kingdom. But you could not swallow her. She was not an object. Now you see the error of your life: trying to swallow everything, unable to let anything out. You see your poems, little maps of the kingdom, showing the new location of the objects you had just swallowed. Now you want to be naked, you want the walls of your body to dissolve into raindrops that fall against the things of this world.

My fear of being swallowed: fear that what I try to do to the world, the world will try to do with me—death, the earth mother. An old children's "song" I remember from sitting on the back porch in Rensselaerville (age 5 or younger) and singing it in a slow chant:

> "I looked at the moon one night.
> The moon looked at me and went ..."

and then making a farting sound by pressing your mouth against your skin and blowing hard. Singing "moon" with two syllables. Sitting in my father's lap. But it also had something to do, maybe a second verse, with being "gobbled up" and then Dad or someone tickled me and I laughed, but in a scared way. It was at night; there was a moon in the sky. "Gobble you up."

Dreams swallow the objects and people of the world, digest and rearrange them in the inner kingdom. Just like my *poems*. My poems are *too much* like dreams in this way. All take and no give, all swallow and digest; no giving back, no giving to others.

¶

1979–1980

December 19: Poetry that does not acknowledge or experience the urge to transcend bores me.

Poetry that yields completely to the urge to transcend frightens me, appalls me (and bores me). The watchword of those who wish to give themselves over to the complete ravishment of transcendence is "purity." Beware that term.

¶

February 12: A lyrical imagination must center itself in the personal, but if the poem goes widely enough, we discover that the personal is merely an inner ring of which the societal and historical are more distant, concentric rings. Under the right circumstances, a poem's scope can include a great number of concentric rings.

¶

February 18: Historical-lyrical flash: That if you, as a poet, are engaged and sustained by the imagination, you must go to Keats' letters, to Coleridge.

If you are responsive to the historical imagination, you should go to Pound's letters.

Pound does not like the Romantics, but more to the point, he does not like or trust imagination. A simple observation to the side: he is a Confucianist—think what position the Chinese Confucianists occupied in relation to their rivals, the Taoists: that tells you where Pound stands.

Perhaps the historical imagination does not like that aspect of imagination which is essential to Keats: the notion of Adam's dream, of imagination itself being creative of truth and beauty. Keats (and Coleridge) give an exalted role to the imagination. Pound does not.

For young poets, Pound is full of good, practical advice. You couldn't get one precise piece of advice from all of Keats' letters. Nevertheless.

¶

March 9: A thought: the failure (of the poem, my poem) is not with the obsession, but with the limitations of the obsession; it's the same old dilemma of personal or private. My obsessions are inherently personal; I must do all I can not to render them private.

¶

June 20: The task of getting back to feeling language inside you, feeling the sounds and rhythms physically. God, that's hard. I feel all this language as being five or ten feet outside me right now—it's getting slowly closer, but it's external; it's like modeling clay or something; it's not inside.

Nor can I transfigure it, or transfigure with it (which is more accurate). Transfigure myself with it.

¶

June 23: Some of my best imagining concerns violence, but for every five violence poems I write, only one succeeds in discovering a larger context or meaning. Unless they do discover this larger context, they become simply a discharge of regressive energy. Even that (a regression) can be made meaningful as in "The Gorge" or (perhaps) "Solitary Confinement." But …

I think I'm inclined to be a little hard on myself about this, too impatient for meanings. Ultimately things will happen—"The Brave Child," which I like a lot, came after at least five years' preparation.

The role of violence in my psyche is not going to be easily resolved. T. points out that my imagination is most vivid when violent.

So much of this morbid, claustrophobic, sensualized violence in my imagination is centered in that life from 12 to 17 or 18 or even later: the horrible sexual desire within and the self-hatred and inhibition all fusing together to form what: a boy who sleeps with his arms crossed on his chest, his feet crossed, like a sarcophagus lid.

I was "raised" to experience and give my assent to the rural American myth of violence as a boy's blood initiation into manhood/malehood. I see this in the most brute form in James Dickey or Robert Penn Warren. But the hunting accident and Peter's death aborted this whole understanding. I think this later joined with my father's alienation from my mother and her suffering to cause me to fail to link up to the second echo of the myth: man versus woman. A myth demands full participation. I couldn't/can't give that to these myths of male power through violence: I think they represent a compensation for our essential human powerlessness; in the face of nature's indifference and the condition of mortality, we have no real power.

That's what I feel/experience. Back to the old story: the terror of existence. I want to acknowledge that terror (I do/the poems do) and I want to set some things, some stories against it (some poems do that—tell stories that are "momentary stays against terror" rather than confusion).

Right now I have in my daily working to confront a lot of unsuccessful poems about the terror and that can be a little depressing. But I must have faith. And patience.

From St. Paul's *Letter to the Corinthians*:
"The Jews seek a sign, and the Greeks seek wisdom."
I'm like the Jews, always seeking a sign, a revelation.

¶

1991

May 10: The horror of Primo Levi's camp stories and the thoughts on the human condition that emerged from his experiences—how I can only take so much of that, then I find myself—as now—reaching for Northrop Frye's essays, which, though occasionally very schematic (as is poetic thought in general, he argues), provides a vision, a transcendent vision that subsumes human suffering to some extent, makes it more bearable. I realize that the mythologies of poetic thought are my "religion"—what makes life bearable to me by integrating personal anguish into a larger scheme—so I am "loosed" in the "pattern's mastery" (to quote an odd, amazing prosepoem of Hart Crane's I encountered yesterday, "Havanna Rose").

Thinking about Levi and Frye I think how my favorite Shakespeare play is *The Winter's Tale*—in large part because it begins in the chaos of tragedy and pivots in the middle into the patterns of romance and rebirth and vegetation myth. It goes from a death-world into a birth-world, an eros world. "It is required you do awake your faith."

How the single, unitary image of the beloved (to meld Nietzsche and Viktor Frankl) is *essential* to the sustenance of my psychic stability.

How destabilized I would feel if the essence of my disease was, as it is with J., promiscuity. I remember that time I was involved with three women at Antioch, or again with several in New York my first year at Columbia—how my sense of identity shattered (ecstatically, perhaps, but definitely shattered—definitely took a deathward turn).

As Frankl (in *Man's Search for Meaning*) said about "love" in the camps: the image of the beloved, "that the poets spoke about," sustained him as nothing else did.

It's a major unitary image behind my "religion"—behind my "religion" of the lyric.

The lyric experience fragments the poet, destabilizes the poet. What restores stability is the possibility of that unitary image, that sustaining symbol.

It needn't always or exclusively be a "beloved" of course, it can also be other things that have become, to borrow Cassirer's borrowed term, "momentary gods."

Someone like Robert Duncan has made a cult of the Beloved, an entire arcane mythology to sustain it—and yet, he has that one ravishing lyric that could itself be worth a lifetime's service: "Often I am Permitted to Return to a Meadow."

❡

May 18: This morning I've flipped over from my "consolidation" mode to my "risk" mode. As I got up this morning I found myself singing the Pointer Sisters' song: "I'm just about to lose control and I think I like it" ("I'm so excited").

Alicia Ostriker

1985

A reading and lecture trip to Oregon, Berkeley, and San Diego

The idea of making love as sticking your tongue
into the calyx of the other & licking up
its nectar, while being licked oneself—
we want this because we are always manufacturing
nectar and when someone sticks a pointy tongue
into us and takes a drop on the tongue-tip and
swallows it   we make more nectar we can
always make more   of our own nectar and
are always thirsty   for the nectar of others

a hustle here & a hustle there
the promiscuous bee

the jostled flower is not devoured
but hums a glucose melody to itself
                    more & more syrupy

The soul selects her own society
should be my motto. I need to travel
around & meet people & pick up their emanations
& have conversations with them & tell each
other our life stories & exchange ideas
& all that, and laugh and get
excited, but I forget most of what they
say, even the good parts, kissing the
joy as it flies—it brushes away on its
wingbeats—what will penetrate me I can
never predict, nor in what form it will
issue: seldom a direct transcription
of the event or the anecdote, phrase,
idea, piece of information—& I wish
I were better at this, I *want* to

bind to myself these joys & make
them my property!

¶

Michael Davidson's best story of the difficult visiting poet: Rexroth demanded that he be provided with   a) a top floor suite in San Diego's best hotel   b) a takahatchi player (this is a difficult Japanese instrument few can play)   c) a koto player (only certain Japanese of aristocratic family background are permitted to play the koto) and   d) either Carolyn Forché or Kathy Acker was supposed to be served up. Michael arranged the other things Rexroth wanted & was then dressed down—in public—for not producing the women for the great old left-winger, he who weeps for Sacco & Vanzetti, etc. "I *love* those women," roared KR.

¶

People seen on plane: a couple of old Jewish people right out of *Tell Me A Riddle*—the husband short, stout & bouncy, saying "God bless you" to the flight attendants; the wife's face a map of brown wrinkles; blind; needing help out of the wheelchair into the plane, & help up the aisle—given by her daughter, middle-aged woman in K-mart clothes (no not quite)

the old woman's hand feeling along the seatbacks as she tries to find her seat in the plane

and being lugged into a wheelchair when we land in Denver—the old man pushes her in—a flight attendant notices she's not all the way in it & will fall—She is mouthing words but I can't understand them because it's a Yiddish accent & because she has no teeth

Two small girls, one blond curly exquisitely beautiful flirtatious & laughing; the sister plainer & in braids; both playing with their small brother

The Borovsky show I saw at Cal Art Museum—loved the painting that was a parody of Moses, all action-painting style messing up the human

Ostriker

figure except for the tablets drawn (cf. Chagall) in outline on a blank space on the canvas they said just one word: sing

¶

The desire of language, the language of desire
The famous masculinity of language which women writers take to be axiomatic: and upon this axiom theory builds its intimidating edifice

Women—learn to recognize when a theory has been organized to intimidate you—learn to question! What do you have this powerful marginal intelligence for? Use it!

We were in Marilyn Farwell's car & her undergraduate student was talking with us about French feminisms. I said: listen—a premise can be a lie. Language isn't monolithic (etc.) Then it struck me—

Language is female. You learned how to speak from a female. As soon as you were born a female began talking to you. Hi there, sweetie. Sweet thing. Sweet love. The female(s) held their face above your face so you could focus on them. They spoke intimately. They held you while they spoke. They were feeding you, undressing and dressing you, washing you. While they did these things they talked. At times they sang. At times they mixed nonsense and sense for the fun of it. You would not be alive if this were not so. Often it is not so & the person dies. They were being playful. They rhymed. Their hands were caressing you, squeezing you, petting you so their arms pressed you to their body. There was a lot of rhythm & a lot of repetition. Language is female. Their arms pressed you to their body. There was smell. Their voices buzzed in your soft ear. They told you that your ear was soft, how delicious your belly, they blew & made farting noises in your belly, they talked, language is female. Language is love. Language is food, clothing, information, immersion in water which frightens you first time then you enjoy it & a towel. You were crying. They were angry. Language is anger. Language is screaming. Language is she hits you. There isn't food. You throw up. Language is she says the things she says it again and again. She says shut up. She says that.

She talks & talks. Do you remember her face when she is talking? She

Ostriker

slaps you. She kisses you she laughs & makes you laugh. You hear a voice, yours. Language is female. Language is female. You hear a smell. Are you embarrassed? Do you remember her face when she is talking? Language is female. Are you embarrassed?

Are you afraid.

Are you afraid if he hears us. Are you afraid to think: LANGUAGE IS FEMALE.

She tells you do this do that. She forbids you. She is talking. She hates you you hate her.

Silence is masculine. Masculinity is silence. He isn't there. He buttons his lip. He keeps a stiff upper lip which makes it difficult to talk. Silence is golden.

He gives orders. Does that make him like her, but more so? He gives her orders (according to the story). He reads the bedtime story. (Like her?)

When he talks it is more important (it says in the story). "But not in *my* family," yells somebody. "Not in *mine*," yells somebody else. (But they don't count, they're ethnic.) She teaches you how to read. She teaches you to write. She teaches you arithmetic. Language is female. Often you are mad at her. You despise her. Language is female. Girls are verbally advanced. Girls do better at reading. Girls do better at spelling. Girls write better. Girls get higher scores on verbal tests and the Educational Testing Service adjusts the method of grading so it will come out even. Language is female. Are you embarrassed? Are you afraid? Don't you want to kiss me?

Logic is male. Theology is male. Philosophy is male. Business is male. Grammar is male. Law is male. Medicine is male. (Healing is female.) The university is male. The church is priests. Where have all the priestesses gone. The *shul* is male. Talmud is male. Uproot her groves. History is male. Mathematics is male. The university is male. War is male. Science is male. Weapons systems are male. "Discourse" is male. If you can draw a line around it it is male. If you can beat somebody with it then it is a symbolic phallus and male and it is might and right.

First of all language is spoken. Then it is written. Then it is printed. Then it is printed-out.

The more dis-embodied the words, the higher their status.

If it is in a book/newspaper, it must be true. Then it is objective.

Then it is dead. The living language is speech, which is constantly regenerated at the core, like the pith of a tree, and the dead language is exhibited on library shelves, collecting dust, like the stationary bark of a tree ... (cf. *Paterson*)

Masculine discourse tries to make you forget a human woman ever held you in her arms & was God. It eliminates agency & responsibility & is abstract as all hell

It is sans teeth, sans eyes—
it is without gesture
it is without facial expression
it is without odor
there is no milk attached to it
it intimidates
it is not necessarily trying to kill you but it does not care
if you live or die

The poem inaugurates/replicates rhythm
    like the things that mama said
        and refrains
The novel includes scenes
people who talk and love
and pain and violent death

When we write, we mean to
communicate so we try to
incorporate in the printed
language the equivalent
of a face, a body, gestures,
a smile, frown, screams an
angry blow—intimacies—

Ostriker

I read the idea of cottage industries
using home terminals is less
successful than anticipated because
          (because we are animals)
because the people with the home
terminals keep coming to the office
where they can sit around and
talk to each other
and people don't just want to
read the journal article or the
book. They want to go to the
conference and hear the colleagues
talk and look at them as best
they can & eat & drink with them

They learn more efficiently that
way, they think … because we are
animals … language is animal

Are you embarrassed?
Are you afraid?

Michael J. Rosen

1983–1991

The mirage depends on our never reaching it; whatever comes within reach has either vanished or proven itself permanent and real and not a mirage at all. As long as we have the illusion of the mirage it remains available, *ours* ... as long as it is unattainable.

In fact, the mirage's most compelling or attractive quality is its very ability to attract. So the mirage is a belief or faith that gives direction towards an illusion that can relieve some present, stressful condition. What's more, like faith, it does not offer confirmation or reassurance. This is exactly what we mean by faith: that which reassures only by its practical inability to offer reassurance. Faith is something strong enough to displace the need for further proof. "Take my word for it," we say, meaning believe in this mirage that I have proposed. Surely this is every poem's pretension: "Reader, take my word for it."

Consider: poetry as a drink at a mirage, an apparent slaking of a thirst, some temporary and imagined relief. This is compatible with the idea that "we have heard it all before" as far as our subjects go, and that a poem is a chance to make us listen, attend, actually hear—be slaked. In that poetry is not a literal occurrence (other than the experience of reading), does it not aspire to the status of a mirage? It offers us its sense of refreshment and revitalization precisely because it exists in the distance, out of reach, on a two-dimensional surface, within an arena withheld from the surfeit of everyday information.

¶

Regarding Matisse's backs or his female busts—those sequential sculptures that progress from realism to abstraction: Over a period of years he removed (by accomplishing each previous version) one layer after another of identifiable physiognomy from the represented forms in order to reveal form of another kind. Likewise, looking at Picasso's bulls, goats, guitars, woman, or so much abstract art—once the viewer's mind is assigned the subject, the eye works to seek this identity, salvaging the corresponding details from the apparent randomness or mystery of abstraction that reason the original or ghost form back into existence. By clinging to that dictated image, by calling out that one noun (goat, face, nude—sometimes only a title offers such an orienting clue), the eye trains itself to reveal what resides (even as residuum) in the artwork.

Just so, in a poem, we learn to observe how "subject" resides beneath contemporary abstractions or manipulations of language, form or narrative. We have the history of literature to suggest how to look, where to search, what to make of what is found.'

How far can such individual manipulations progress before the exactions upon the reader overwhelm the derived pleasures, before the readerly conventions of expectation, recognition, pleasure, etc., are flouted and the poem must survive (dazzle, daze) on its own uncanny nature?

Can form be a result of the distance between some ideal portrayal of a given reality (something delimited and disrupted by the onset of utterance) and the acceded terms of abstraction an individual finds to convey it, however inadequately? (Think of the necessary abstraction in a painting's staffage—its smaller components, incidentals, auxiliary characters that do not warrant the focus and precision; think of the most realistic painter's approximations for multitudes—a crowd's faces, leaves, grass.) Something, some form, in every case *strains* material (to cull and to call into crisis) into a comprehensible sufficiency. Form is that intercession, that narrowing of focus and dissembling of nature that is applied to the nearly infinite realities that comprise any given view. Form as a necessary act of metonymy.

¶

The better question to be asked by the curious enough student or the general reader: Not "Where do you get your ideas from?," but "How do you keep your ideas from you?" The answer, then, is comprised of all the ways we defeat our natural inclination to trot out our tiresome ideas, launch our current diatribes. To rely confidently on the fact that our ideas are the least reticent, least difficult elements to bring to bear in a poem. They insinuate, encroach, inhere especially if we pay them no mind. The hard thing is to find a small enough, peculiar enough context in which such ideas actually matter, actually govern (without pretention, oversimplification, or cavalier presumption) a knowable universe. To give an idea a true test, rather than the trial runs that compose our conversations, letters, journalism.

⁋

Form is the running of interference: one thing (contraption, semi-permeable membrane) I put between myself and my idea, between me and others, between writer and reader; one thing that provides the blocking (tackling the likely defenses to the idea) so that the poem's central figure can reach the goal.

This is interference against my own expeditious, inspired, urgent tendencies to succumb to the momentum of style, to *complete*. This is, too, interference against the sated reader who is ready to skim, to turn the page.

If art (let's confine this to writing) were merely the appropriation of all the right techniques, skills, data, etc., (in photography: the mastery of the camera), the best writing should come from the most skilled practitioner of the medium (the best photographs from the perfectly able operator of the camera).

We know this is not the case: Something impedes, interferes, tangles with such notions of perfect execution. (More likely, we come to recognize that "perfect execution" yet depends on a human agent, and that notions of perfection are themselves multiple and responsive to a range of human intentions. Still, I only wish to establish this cold, cerebral idea of perfection in order to establish this interference.)

Perhaps the first problem is that desire for perfection—accuracy, documentation, realistic depiction—is an impossibility itself, for those qualities are so impossible to render as to demand convention for their very apprehending. What we call "style" and "voice" and "vision" must be the lens—the interferences—which brings into focus, into reach, any possible reading of a given situation, any excerpt from the infinite undertaking of perception.

The limitations of a "voice" in poetry (what it cannot do, where it cracks, strains—"the grain of the voice"), these are as creditable to the poet and as credible as the voice's lushness, articulateness, polish. Voice, then, being that combination of attained and unattained elements that creates an adequacy for a given use.

The problem of adequacy. A pet peeve: reading poetry where the writer has managed to shuck enough humility to believe that what is being written is truly a sufficient explanation of the subject. How impoverished everything we write must be. How often can we actually explain ourselves (our actions, desires, problems) to ourselves—to the point of ever being said and done with the subject, so done with it that we don't feel the temptation to bring it up again in conversation … let alone in a poem? How often can we adequately explain ourselves to others? How much more difficult when a second party is involved—all the motivations of individual readiness, need, compassion, history, etc., must link together in the exchange. Then how can a poet give a poem the unreasonable and bombastic expectation of ultimate communication—a summary-like, know-it-all affect that proudly admits "now you have heard it" *and* you'll never need to hear it again. The fact is that we are Sisyphean in our need to hear everything again; we are unable to listen in a way that makes the world's lessons perfectly applicable to all present and future situations, and we require the repeated attempt. (There it is: the idea of the unattainable, the mirage, as the means that suffices for the end.)

Perfection, once again, does not provide—it will not continue to apply and must be generated each time within a given context. Voice, style, context, form—these are the mismanagements, abstractions, conventions, idiosyncrasies, that enable each of us to present a graspable, realistic aspect of the infinite realities offered our perceptions. These are the means we have of selecting a subject from the human arena (the "all" of "we've heard it all before"), and rendering it in a poem that we can listen to over and over and never hear well enough to forget.

¶

Rosen

As with a body's physiological immune system, we each develop conceptual antibodies to combat potential ideas, experiences, emotions that could undermine our happiness. Instead of our immune system's immunoglobulins, blood cells, etc., our minds generate their own battalion: impatience, satiety, and judgment with its dismissive arsenal of labels such as *sentimental, disingenuous, derivative, precious*.

A poem is one sensibility invading another, the writer's work encountering a reader's resistance. (Some readers have a natural immunity to poetry that effectively safeguards the reader from any response; some have weakened resistance; some, clearly, are so susceptible that the only relief seems to be self-expression rather than poetry.) Therefore the object is to introduce a new strain, to affect a new susceptibility—to offer an antigen for which the reader has no ready defense, no well-rehearsed mechanism to neutralize and eliminate, no built-up response to greet the poem and (with like-minded recognitions) render it harmless. The difficulty is, each time, to inject some known subject (they are all known), in a state that is altered enough (a nuance of an idea in a specific context) so as to escape another's homeostatic forces of resistance, refusal, disinterest and to cause a reaction. A physical reaction. To be moved, we say ... as in to mobilize the forces of a genuine reaction.

¶

In a poem, two axes: the x-axis of the literal, reality, plot, event, and the y-axis of the imaginative, thematic, meditative, philosophical. Each aspect of a poem possesses these two coordinates that can describe its position in the poem. Each line has a storytelling, forward, horizontal momentum that records what is occurring (what happens next), and a meditative, pausing, vertical momentum that records the effect of such progress upon the speaking sensibility (what's happened?).

Faults with a poem: when one or the other component approaches 0? With no narrative motion, the emotion (sentimentality) or imagination (fantasy) zooms high above the page. With nothing but narrative (journalism?), there is but the horizontal ploddiness of exposition.

Could the coordinates also be labeled action (x-axis) and passion (y-axis)? Recall from the introduction to Aristotle's *Poetics*: *Action*: active; the psyche perceives something it wants and moves toward it. *Passion*: passive; the psyche suffers something it cannot control or understand and is "moved" by it.

¶

The expression, "No rhyme or reason for that," means to suggest two possible arenas—the illogical and the logical—for a given action. The "or" implies that these are two difference guesses, that between the two must exist a vast divide, exhausted in the effort of determining the motive for whatever the phrase referred to. Neither a reason (logical, the action-oriented motion toward desire?) nor a rhyme (the passive, the opposite pole in the field, the acted upon?).

Need we accept the notion that reason and rhyme must exhibit contrary values and uses, inhabit different worlds, perhaps overlapping only accidentally in coincidence? (From Auden's "Horae Canonicae," Part 4, "Nones": "What we know to be not possible/Though time after time foretold .../Or revealed to a child in some chance rhyme/Like will and kill, comes to pass/before we realize it."

If only to elevate rhyme to the status of reason. To construct simultaneously cogent, unexpected, accurate, meaningful, and still satisfying rhymes. How many poems possess the ability to go beyond aural pleasure, mnemonic tidiness, ludic pleasures, and actually construct ongoing sound sense with their rhymes?

¶

Tangent: Difference between lyric and narrative: The lyric is akin to cetacean communication: the whale or dolphin's broad simultaneity of frequencies presented within the briefest temporal sequence. The result is a concentration of diverse and singular elements expressed at once. A vertical poem, that does not require accumulation. Less order than revolution. More committed to rereading, the return.

Rosen

The narrative poem possesses the large temporal component like human communication. A small number of possible sounds arranged in a lengthy distribution of speech. The plot of words—which came first and which came after. Reliance on time and the recapitulation of things in a significant and revealing order. More committed to the single reading, the continuation.

¶

A poem is the shape of disquietude. It is written by the one who wakes, who leaves the bed in order to think further in the non-narrative arena of the morning's earliest hours. The poem is proof, left for the one who wakes later. It is an assembled hope of shared recognition for the one who, protected by sleep, managed to forgo or forget the threatening moment of awareness.

We are all asleep while someone is writing about something we have forgone or forgotten.

Though the poet is not always rising from bed to write, the occasion of writing is nevertheless one of private concentration, a secluded preparation for the sake of oneself and for another. The poem is, by definition, "after the *fact*"—meaning, something created later as a result of the fact. So what is given to the sleeper, now awake and reading, is not a fact of the world but the poet's interpretation or manipulation of such evidence. The supererogatory nature of the poem presumes that every reader is asleep. An aggressive, arrogant, alarming act: To rouse the reader to the poem's occasion.

Liz Rosenberg

1986

I've been thinking about my own generation, what we were as teenagers: a watchful decade; aloof, observant, suspicious, self-absorbed, compassionate, uncertain, hopeful and cynical by turns. Our great weapon was humor, as against the largely humorless 60s, the ambitious 80s. We saw the flower children fail, and empathized with our parents—we waited to see what would happen. Mostly we're still waiting.

❧

The graduate office at the university: wicker pencil holder in the shape of a dog, thousand-year-old mints in a white dish. Women with short dark hair and a notorious bobby pin, a plastic red rose or pink carnation in a white plastic vase. The poets will never be welcome or at home here.

❧

Stories or poems—Van Gogh's brother, Freud's attachment to & defense of then recanting of cocaine, the story of Mrs. Washington Roebling who lost son & husband to the building of the Brooklyn Bridge & then finished it herself.

❧

The student poets came creeping into the auditorium, all of them wearing black clothes—most of them in long black coats. And a shadow fell over the audience.

❧

Fiction requires a certain accumulation or weight to work. First paragraph is proposition for the story and last seals it off.

❧

Emily Dickinson *cuts into* her poems with a welder's arc. If there's a daintiness in that, think of the strength and agility required!

❧

How shall we let the dead bury the dead? When we all know it's the dead who bury the living!

❡

Of John [Gardner]—I am thinking of Dave Smith's charge against him that he had no sense of humor—and of the outlandish, clownish dances he used to perform with just his feet—lying on his back in the living room listening to music. It was elegant and comic to see those clodhopper boots move like whole dancers—it was Chaplinesque. But everything he did was art.

❡

1987

Last Sat. took a pregnancy test and to my amazement—delight, awe, a touch of horror—found it positive. Occasional drowsiness, like a fit of vapors. Feel too as if I am racing against time on my own work—as if I were in low-lying land and could feel the fog rolling in.

❡

A hero is one who in the face of danger pushes the highest elements in himself to the maximum limit. Isabel Archer—bravery and commitment to truth, confronting Madame Merle. Shackleton's bravery, endurance and stewardship in Antarctica. Always in heroism there is the presence of actual physical danger or of failure.

❡

Crazy Eddie on TV, making faces at the camera, his face all bloated and distorted saying, "Crazy Eddie's prices are INSANE" & his eyes are little & cunning & greedy & so shameless you realize he really *is* insane.

❡

Van Gogh's painting of the asylum—he gets the medicine-y colors & feeling of desolate space—in the arches. If you have vision, everything else takes care of itself. With art one is always thinking, what a simple, what a wonderful solution! As in Van Gogh's rain— blue lines.

¶

This is the way I am, my husband opposite. We see an old couple doddering down the street, he says, how nice, look how long they've been together while I say in the same breath, Look how old they are. Soon they'll die and have to lie apart.

¶

Cormorant on a lake stump. A most flexible and ever-moving neck, velvet black back & large spread wings with gray tatters like the old coat of an elegant aging gentleman. He points with his neck—I suppose constantly searching for food. Japanese grace and absurd balance. It seems his wings would ache from holding them outstretched like that. The way some people do.

¶

Most important, Eli [son] is here, sleeping peacefully in the plastic hospital bassinet to my left, the image of perfection, hands folded toward his mouth. A baby is like a poem—self-absorbed and containing in himself the universal breath, and needing constant tiny cares & adjustments.

¶

At a poetry reading. First night out alone without Eli or David— dreamy and gone, as if on drugs. Looking around at this carpeted university room, full of students in blue jeans, so much alike, so bedimmed of their animal joy. I remembered the Sufi expression, A pregnant woman is always right and thought: A new mother never lies. So I see this place clear, for once. God help us! We're writing in a dead language. And I can't stand to think that Eli will ever learn to be muffled, polite like this. We write a poetry of the cultured—we should be writing out into the street, down into the earth.

¶

I see my reflection like a passing cloud speeding over the faces of students eating their lunch. The boy with missing hand. A man with bloody eyebrow brilliant red. The multiforms of humanity, the grown-up babies walking past me.

¶

Two men in restaurant talking about wine—a valiant wine, bold, courageous yes but unpretentious, vital, straight-forward, virile. The men are crazy, of course.

¶

Last lines of poems—complete yet kinetic.

¶

I wish that everyone would look at me with eyes like the eyes my newborn son has in his head.

¶

Is post-modernism an extension—another phase of modernism—or a break with it? Most literary periods defined by wars. Consider the kinds of wars and you'll see the differences in the literature.

¶

It's never too late to rise up & be a flame. It's not too late as long as you're breathing, as long as your eyes are jerking back and forth the lovely way they do, reading. It's never too late to stop wasting your life.

¶

1988

Eli eight months old today—sitting upright for the first time as we stroll, a fine spring day, cool and sunny and green.

¶

The hours I wanted to escape from teaching, or took my break in a dark empty classroom—the fumblings, the wise thing almost said when headache or phone call intervened. The dying woman who interrupted my class with her pale face—not till after the funeral did I understand her urgency to thrust at me a few last poems. *I Dreamt I Dwelt in Marble Halls*—which is a song about death.

¶

Feeling really dismal—out of proportion gloom. Iron-cold weather, both of our cars dead at once. The day shot—about to go get Eli from sitter. "How small is that with which we struggle; how great that which struggles with us." Rilke.

¶

1989

In Wilson Hospital Intensive Care Unit, Eli asleep in the stainless steel crib attached to tubes, resting more comfortably tonight. Gurgle & hiss of the tubes a white noise. Watching the red numbers of his pulse monitor, the green waves of his heartbeat like a man running or Hebrew letters forming right to left. I am thinking about Eli—and myself—and how though I think of myself as a good mother I am impatient—covetous of my own time and work. What am I doing that's so important or wonderful? When I have all this time to sit here, I sit and stare at him or at his monitors.

¶

Funny how you learn to live with hospital sounds—soft ringing and bleeps and hissing—and to live by shifts, waiting for the nice nurse to come on, dreading the shift of the cranky ones like the reign of a bad king. You learn to live in eight-hour clumps—all three of them. About half the people in medicine shouldn't be here—doctors and nurses who are harried, brittle, bitter, sharp-tongued, lazy, indifferent, clumsy, resentful—and the other half are geniuses. We have had more good than bad. But you occasionally see the nurses who just want to sit in the nurse's station and eat or talk on the phone, or flirt with the young male doctors in an almost-motherly way, putting their arms around them and laughing a lot. Nurses who say everything in a loud piercing voice as though illness were distance and you had to raise your voice to shout over it.

¶

The peaceful, even sound of Eli's breathing fills the car. This is my work time, while he naps, but I know if I bring him upstairs he'll wake up and probably not get back to sleep again.

¶

I write for insomniacs, grievers, depressives, lonely-hearts, hopefuls and children. I wouldn't say that I write in order to comfort or distract them, exactly—but to give a voice to what is already in them that needs a voice.

Also I write in order to make God repent of His sins.

¶

I turn away from some acquaintance, laughing inanely, only to hear my two-year-old echo my nervous chuckle, his arm lifted like mine in some half-assed gesture of farewell, his shoulders hunched like a whining beggar. Better to bite the woman on the shoulder or wrap my arms around her legs and wail, or toss a ball at her head and run, or say to her "Move!" or "Don't go!" or "Go!" but never to make a liar of this vibrant creature tripping at my heels picking up scraps of every lunacy I drop behind.

¶

In the midst of this nothing then, something—like the light rising off the day, a green mist. To fear the earth is not to stop loving it. Darkness, if not nowhere then everywhere—no one else on earth is so extreme except for man, so extremely anxious to get off it, to get on with it, to name everything with a word and so tame it with his ferocity.

¶

The truth is maybe somewhere in between, in glimmering.

※

This is someone's real name: True Willing Laughing Life Bucky Boomerang Manifest Destiny.

※

1990

How do you expect me to work like this? You clumsy oaf of a god—how could anyone have thought you were a woman? You don't give a damn about children, injustice, the world—it's all a green ghost to you.

You wait to be served, hold out your empty plate, your pipe, your boots on the back of my neck bowed over a book. Are you listening to me, damn it?

I'm talking to myself again.

※

The endurance of vision—the significance of details—the importance of good directions.

※

Sometimes the day opens out like an alley of green lights up ahead.

※

1991

Three is the age of independence for Eli. He can walk, run, climb, slide alone and this allows him to enter his own world. What's gruelling, early on, is when one must follow along behind endlessly, watching out, rescuing and worrying—constantly centered on the child's world which is to an adult often boring or silly —a good thing in small doses, but not a constant diet, not to entirely usurp the privacy of one's own adult world—thoughts and ideas, observations, feelings or sensations. This

I consider a fundamental human right. Even ritualized religion, in its rituals, allows for private prayer.

¶

Blink and it's 11:30 at night—always. No matter how early you start the evening. Have been thinking—any time a parent makes a child cry in an emotional situation, that's probably the parent's mistake. But the strength and stamina and patience to find another way, that's the hard part. It helps if you close your eyes and just listen to the child's voice. The wild faces and gestures are distracting. I sometimes think the voice is the most honest organ of the body. If there is any way to see a child more clearly, it's to *hear* him.

¶

Have instituted a month-long plan to buy nothing that isn't vital (food, medicine) or maintenance (batteries, etc.) Also to stop all selling of self—writing for money, submitting work. Just to see what could happen if I remove myself from all that—to see what's left. Not to buy or order or covet or browse. Tremendously hard work—laying waste our powers becomes a habit of thinking and doing.

¶

Sitting in rectangle of white sun, in quiet house, very happy. The ball-point pen makes a star of light against the shadow of my hand moving across the page below. Happy for once to *be*.

¶

For me, motherhood is all wild swings up & down—exhilaration, then crushing boredom, adoration or fury, delight then frustration—sometimes both at once. To be a mother seems to require subsuming one's self—and that is what's so hard, especially in art.

My friend Sheila said, When I do have 5 minutes alone to myself I don't know what to do anymore, how to think like an adult. My mind's a blank.

I remember that feeling so well—having nearly escaped it I feel I've escaped a jail. "I would give up the inconsequentialities for my children—my money, my life—but I would not give up my self." Edna Pontellier—THE AWAKENING.

Recall Betsy Aswad's good advice—get an hour alone, no matter what you have to do to get it.

The problem being that an hour is not enough. Not for art. Maybe not even to regain one's right mind.

¶

Realized tonight—I no longer expect that anything I do will turn out a success. Whatever one does. It vanishes, like throwing a stone into a deep well. Or a scrap of paper. You don't even see it or hear it sink but you know it's sunk. And then your life fills up with stuff to disguise the emptiness. Is there poetry in silence?

¶

One can rush through a whole day—month after month—without one single moment of quiet thought or reflection. So it goes with me. Fear & anger are the enemies of art.

But I also thought today, if one could just write without them, anything would be possible.

Vern Rutsala

August approaches and some work has been done and some is there to be finished. The secret is pace and rhythm—I think. If we were lathes we could turn out lovely lines by the hour but we aren't. And can't. The lines have a way of waiting. The occasions lurk within the days and hours. We say, with Baudelaire, that inspiration is working every day and want to believe it. And we do try to work every day but we know that things build up, some backlog in the senses or deeper, some artesian well of the psyche is there and the day comes when we draft six new poems. This isn't like working every day. This isn't diligence. Something else is at work—some calibrator we don't even want to begin to fathom is at work. The best we can do is say thank you to our private dust bowl muse and wonder, like cavemen greeting a new spring, if it will ever happen again—and begin the revisions.

¶

Little of the past is in color and most of it has only two dimensions. As we remember we pluck up people like paper dolls—paper dolls we try to turn into balloons by breathing life into them. Sometimes they flush a bit with color—a faint pastel—and seem to want to grow but mainly they stay flat and black and white.

The past is always a little behind you, over your left shoulder, until you look.

¶

Did the obsession begin when I watched my mother writing a letter? I remember the awe I felt as the cursive letters flowed out so neatly and quickly across the page. I remember thinking—will I ever be able to do that? I was five or six. I had similar feelings watching my father draw and wanted somehow to wear his hand like a glove and draw that well too.

¶

American version of Brecht: First the porkchops, then the mashed potatoes.

¶

Those people we saw last night were like figures erased from a blackboard, faintly seen through the chalk dust. They wanted to assert themselves but there was too little to them—only those dim lines and suggestions of personality like connect-the-dot pictures.

¶

Overheard: "We checked out the bars of which there was two."

¶

Spender was in town: A number of us were talking about Yeats' habit of writing out prose versions of his poems and then turning them into verse. We prattled out a number of theories and then time collapsed when Spender said he remembered what Yeats had said—here was history rearing up!—and how Yeats said there still had to be something of the "We'll go no more aroving" in even the prose. This was astonishing—not the statement but the fact that what had been, only a few moments before, literary history—the kind you grow up with—suddenly became living history and we were linked with Yeats for an instant by means of Spender's memory.

I remember Lowell greeting Spender in the ICA lobby in London: "Hi, Steve," he said and it didn't sound right. This was STEPHENSPENDER, all one word and part of history, too.

¶

Amichai: In answer to someone who asked where in his work was "the perspective of eternity, the grand vision of Moses and the prophets, the sense of divine purpose pulsating in the movements of history?"

His answer: "What you are insisting on, what you are looking for in poetry, is exactly the sort of phony phraseology with which the generals and ideologues and politicians pollute our verbal atmosphere. It's precisely against this that a poet has to take his stand, for the job of a poet is to name each thing, each feeling, each experience, plainly and accurately, without pretense." Three cheers!

¶

Rutsala

At a party someone said something about Russians killing their poets. I said but here we let them kill themselves.

¶

Marianne Moore: "Discouragement is a form of temptation…" It's always there, saying give up, call it quits. Sticking with it is a matter of character or stupidity or necessity. Or maybe a thick skin. No one asks us to write but there are many things that tell us not to—rejection near the top of the list. There are worse things than doggedness. In fact Moore quotes Pound: "The great writer is always the plodder; it's the ephemeral writer that has to get on with his job."

¶

Sincere love poems aren't good. Good love poems aren't sincere.

¶

Existentialism is no longer fashionable but that doesn't mean the abyss has disappeared.

¶

For most Americans history is what you had for dinner last night or the movie you saw. Or maybe it only goes as far back as breakfast.

¶

That time many years ago when I flew to Portland from Iowa City: Over Idaho I looked down and there, in the middle of winter and looking absolutely dead under the ice and snow was McCall—I was certain of it. The town where I was born and spent my first eight years. Yes, there it was outside and below. I was flying to Portland because my father was having his first operation for cancer. In the plane and looking down I wanted time to slow up and somehow melt all that below me so we could get back to those times. But it was like the past, still and frozen and impossible to reach. I craned to look as long as I could and then it was pulled away and gone. I've spent years trying to get back there.

¶

Wittgenstein: "If a lion could speak we would not understand him."

❡

Title: *Faute de mieux*.

❡

A Yorkshire couple were engaged for forty years and finally one said, "We really should get married." The other answered, "But who would have us?"

❡

British names: Jeremy Sprid Cote; Lady Margaret Vane-Tempest Stewart; Bickham Sweet-Escott; Bamber Gascoigne; Lisa St. Aubern de Teran; and there is the journalist, Perigrine Worsthorne whose real name is Koch de Gooneynd. An American would change his name to Smith or as my uncles did, from Rutsala to Russell. This is another reason we have so little in common with the British.

John Huston's favorite British name: Lord Dominick Oranmore and Browne.

❡

Bad news: the popularity of such words as parenting, interface, networking, lifestyle, supportive, impact as a verb. Without such words many people nowadays would be mute. So be it.

❡

Somerset Maugham: "We *believe* the earth is round; we *know* it is flat."

❡

It's snowing. The street is transformed. A small inkling of delight begins to nudge into the night. All the everyday dullness is being covered and the street becomes white metaphor. "Life is more interesting than we had been lead to believe."

Rutsala

The memory of that icy time when our street was frozen and high school kids played hockey on it under the streetlights. The strangeness of it, their long gliding movements, the quiet except for the sound of the skates.

¶

Chamfort: "Society is made up of two great classes: those who have more dinners than appetite, and those who have more appetite than dinners."

There is also the one about the rich and the poor getting their fair share of ice: The rich in summer, the poor in winter.

E. Elliott:
    The law locks up the man or woman
    Who steals the goose from off the common;
    But lets the greater villain loose
    Who steals the common from the goose.

¶

That clergyman in the Philippines called Cardinal Sin!

¶

Lines, ideas:

The smell of oil and gas …
Bob's strutting skinny walk …
The lake bulging …

Those night feelings …
A swirl of mica in cosmic dust,
dimensions wholly changed …
Feelings of pettiness about *our* things …

¶

Rutsala

Enthusiasm is one of the most repugnant human qualities—in others. We, of course, wear it lightly and manage it with enormous grace.

¶

We need that absence of self-consciousness of the ancient Chinese poets. It takes skills we don't seem to have to write poems which are simply invitations to have a drink.

¶

Saints shouldn't gag when they kiss lepers.

¶

Adhering too strictly to a set form is like dancing in a closet.

¶

Too many American writers are as guilty of anti-intellectualism as the general populace. They boast of how they don't read, they take pride in their stupidity. It's a matter of taking on protective coloration but it's a lousy act. As Sartre pointed out years ago: To care in America is to be one of the damned.

Artists, pro's, also-rans. This is the right order.

¶

There is also the problem of the middle class sensibility. It gives people the most severe set of blinders ever invented. If you're trained while young not to see certain things you will never see them unless you make a profound effort. There was that student's story—how his mother told him not to look when they drove by the poor part of town.

¶

Lines:

Fish nibbling at the bait of the moon
resting on the surface...

Rutsala

Outside, the poor wander by
with broken toys—our largesse—
which no one fixes ...

¶

The natural world is near, out there in the back yard in fact. Blackberries and weeds, a sterile holly tree, twine and swirl like a kind of green surf. It has taken over the yard and you feel it wants the house, to make the wood come home ...

¶

On a Photograph of William Carlos Williams and Ezra Pound:

Williams is seated and Pound stands behind him with his hands on Williams' shoulders as if holding him up. Their postures suggest the ventriloquist and his dummy for while Pound's lips are tightly sealed Williams' mouth is open and he seems to be speaking. Or have they posed this way to reinforce or mask an early theory, i.e., that Pound was behind Williams? Or are things reversed and are Williams' lips moving because he is a poor ventriloquist and Pound's lips sealed because he is a poor dummy? Clearly it is a puzzling picture. One may wonder as well why Pound has his shirt draped over his shoulders, cape-like, or why both seem to smile just slightly. Is there some joke involved? But who is in on it?

¶

Amid hard cold rain and snow we left for Gatwick. Arrived in good time. Again the idea of "Airport Scenes" struck me. There's a kind of nakedness and show of feeling at airports that is rarely public. The theater of departures and arrivals. The many family dramas. (Overheard: "I tried to calm her down but it was no use.") Like hospitals they're at the spiritual center of our age. Spiritless cathedrals. Those high ceilings ...

Peter Sacks

1991

Cape Town, May 12: The fire mantling behind closed eyes. And then the fire itself. Always that margin and excess, upleaping, chewing at the wood, whatever's cut and dried burned back to the glowing scroll, the dead mouth hissing backward to intolerable pain: speaking out of where we go, the journey out of nature? deeper in? and of the catching up? while all around—above this tearing, ripping—images of peace. The first stars coming out like thorns.

What is the fire?

Bees in the heather, and the surf below. Why not be drugged and carried downward by the sounds toward a hive of their own making? Yesterday, after seeing [my father] in the hospital, I drove out to the beach and swam out past the waves to deeper quieter waters where the ocean swung and held me. To the body's pain and question, give only the body's wordless answer lulled and carried in the melting light.

Not that such an "answer" calms the question or the need:

—new growths in the spinal cord so that he's paralyzed from the waist down, spontaneous fractures in the back and shoulder; and everywhere the skin so thin it breaks like tissue, unable to hold him up for washing without breaking the skin, worrying we'll break more bones …

perhaps it simply makes a shore-like point of meeting—wash and friction—where our pain and ignorance and *lack of faith* meet something equally pressing, huge, but indifferent and absorptive, not differentiated and piercing. Wide instead of narrow, narrow, narrow. Doesn't *anguish* at its origin mean narrow, straits?

¶

May 13: Asked him what he'd read in the paper: "violence, violence, slaughter, burning … *terrible* bloody business," rolling his rrs—this morning's pre-dawn raid in Swanieville, the hostel "dwellers" rampage through the shantytown, 27 dead, the photo of a corpse left in the street, a charred arm stiffly raised, the left arm, charred club of the hand … For what? rivalry for an approaching power, the who gets what?

Sacks

or sheer ecstatic rage, ecstatic grief—a bleeding woman screaming out her grief and terror by her husband's corpse: Mrs. Elsie Mvokwe, blood trickling from beneath her *doek*, would not go to the hospital until the corpse had been removed—if no sudden mutuality then a harder butchering, more killed in this violence than in opposition to the government, easier to risk and squander life in this rampaging fury (even if manipulated by "third force") than in deliberate resistance/revolution; sheer rage vengeful and exultant (or just grimly satisfied to settle accounts or to provoke another matching rage and grief)—killing those who share a misery that's now become intolerable, a furious attempted speeding up of change, the self-annihilation from despair—from deprivation, crowding, living in a world of trash, to war against these consequences not the far off cause?

and looked up *anguish*, kin to anger, hence to grief, and ancient words for strangle. The "answer" gives us breath so pain and doubt have something still to choke. So the torturer: Sigaret? And the walls take in the smoke.

altar, sacrifice: smoke ascending mediates between the realms, they said, earth and heaven, man and god. I say between the pained and the indifferent. Before his time, Cain's knowledge, reaching for the stone. Why is the first murder in scripture tied to a rejected sacrifice?? What if both had been accepted, or both rejected? Why should the differentiation—great enough to provoke a brother-murder—be via sacrifice? Why is it Cain's descendants who invent the instruments of music? How to know what Cain knows and be *kind*—not murderous, exclusive, moving always in a rage, the forms of anguish? Abel knows what Cain knows.

For the poet now, i.e. since the death of sacrifice, is form itself the figure and the work of anguish? Such that even free verse or the varying opennesses are ways of breathing whose apparent freedom and release exist only as functions of the stranglehold? the smoke, the screen, the blind. and then the fire.

I used to think the lyric was a way of altering the breath so that we could be alive and dead at the same time, the time of poetry—

breathing and posthumous, body and acknowledged spirit; that poetic form might be death's homeopathic cure and exorcism of the death instinct. Something more uncanny than memorial. Why even think about it now he's in such pain?

Because I want to think about sacrifice, the way an earlier generation wanted to think about God after the supposition of His death. About sacrifice because I know two kinds of certainty without knowing how to connect them: of anguish—his dying, the country's trouble, the natural world's; and of joy, whose stubborn wildest inner-outer reach is one of blessed reverence, touched by something that is at once greater than the self and that feels at moments benign, recoverable in still greater fullness, a (religious?) joy—whence immortality, political hope (to change the human heart), our chance of rescuing the earth. The two can't be convincingly connected just by an aesthetic strategy or form, unless these mark some prior hinging function such as sacrifice? And held by the community as effective. Not scapegoating, not private magic.

From this comes my present difficulty with writing at all, especially writing for others *of my own time*. [What if the old sense of fame (an audience in posterity)(or for me altered, posthumous breath) were merely the side-effect of an unbearable, in many ways disabling, and self-isolating rage and grief *and* joy, as these issue through a medium that is itself inhuman?]

And so this increase of notebook work (and decrease of all other writing), which is somehow *not* yet in that state of tension/issuance, but which exists partly in the hope of opening the door to poetry, of accelerating towards it. Not yet, because lacking the *hinge* that lets the door swing between anguish and curative joy. If the hinge were once a kind of sacrificial procedure, and if my sense of lyric and of any poetics can't free itself from that origin, then part of my work now to continue writing will be to find-form-invent-undergo a credible experience of sacrifice that is as true to pain as it is to joy, while capable of transformatively linking the former to the last. For me now suffering has lost its meaning, while my joy is of a weird, unhinged nature, one which has no grip on pain, and which defines itself by utter distance from whatever circumstances give me time, space, inner life, to feel something beyond circumstance; and one whose far out solitude feels too selfish even in its apparent shedding of the self. Unless by such (*such* is the give-away, metaphor—the symbolic transfer broken down: the poet may now have to act, as well, beyond poetry to satisfy this part of the call and free the other, though where's the line?) unless by such an act of surrender (as poet's to poem, force, will, call-past-self), be it via pain *or* joy, the knife will strip you of whatever seems to keep you from still greater life, and thence: a dying person feels past agony and death the quantum in us that can't die, feels recognized as such; those with the power to oppress share from a recognition of what we all share, radical and sentient as breath; we take the weight of our greed off the planet, source.

I can't write without worrying about this—to do so would risk impoverishing my notion of what poetry does; though again, when the stuff comes, the rest of this gets sidelined though it's no doubt *pressing on the line*, pressing from a region that's then almost unconscious, since conscious and unconscious will have nearly traded places. I can't write poems out of worry, though I can worry *between* poems as now. Worry. The word's odd enough (why now?) to look up; it too goes back to *strangle*! So perhaps that was all or half-wrong up there about anguish and the forms of poetry etc. When truly writing, no matter what the grief or anger, I'm writing also (maybe *only*) out of joy? no poem without the hinge, tho' it's there on its own terms. So why theorize about the act of writing as if I were buying the poem rather than being given it?!

Dante re joy, the form of surrender-sacrifice that is joy itself. How else start *Paradiso* with Marsyas as figure of received inspiration! Flayed by Apollo. And later, in the sphere of Venus, *per letiziar lassu folgor s'acquista / si come riso qui,* by joy up there brightness is won, just as by a smile on earth; but down below the shade darkens externally as the mind saddens. And *Non pero qui si pente, ma si ride*—i.e. not repent but smile. All as if joy might be a form of return, of reascent. Not penitence but joy. Dante's graduated ascent, every step or flight upward brought about by part of his belief; and the entire *Paradiso* constantly about the smile.

And now recall Dad saying to me (strange how he went back to Afrikaans, as if more intimately rooted there) *"Moenie so lyk nie. Jy moet glimlag."* Don't look like that (here he mocked my frown). You must smile.

And then *his* smile.

[*folgor*, a flashing flame, as lightning out of thundercloud]

His room open to the garden, lawn, oaks, flowers, sweeping breeze. Just now sleeping: downturned mouth opening to a dark inverted horseshoe, hands crossed over the swollen belly, covering the plastic bell-switch; voices from the corridor—Xhosa flowing over English words wheelchair, bunny blanket, trolly, we're just going to do her dressing; and Afrikaans natuurlik, nou-nou, vreeslik—tinkle of a teaspoon in a glass, his light snore draining, draining; a train accelerating out of Kenilworth. Not he, *You*, father, it's only you this moment, how existence all of it heaps over you, a concentration of intensity but without meaning.

In the breeze a dead moth, upturned, rocked on the linoleum. I'm wondering how to draw the line: will your dying and your death now be associated with *everything*? Should there be borders? Death's full tide over the shore, the current rocking, turning to the spiral of what sinks. They called the hoist above you a monkeychain—a short trapeze hung from its hook. Watch fastened like a gold crab on your wrist.

leafage of the creeping rose, the stems tied spiralling around veranda columns, new growth leaning outward, leaf-veins branching. And a blown leaf hops across the lawn. leafage of the creeping rose, pressed on me, for the having, like a reassurance though I can't say why—new life aging in *one* season, shadows drifting on the brick.

where do my impulses begin? out of the remembered land? leafage, creeping rose. What says breathe deeper, or brings me to the image of

Sacks

long oarstrokes and the water moving backward in wide reaches—leaf and leafshadow now stripped of you or me or any of us, riding mingled with the wake?

beauty in the natural world, the breath I breathe—love for this life despite the knowledge now never more pressing of the body's self-betrayal; of being part of this, composed of it, dying back into it, soil of the rock, and of the mountains all around these seas, the lives brief as the flare and sinking of a struck match, white-caps on the sea, knowing here within these words some trace of salt, of mineral, tide-line, and avowal, you now riding this—and we who follow soon, waves further out but travelling after, unrepeatable but following the same fate, the part that gathers carries what it can—our calling is our unique way of breaking

oil of autumn, hooded wisdom of the flesh
oil of the lamp, unhooded wisdom of the flesh

and then that single stirring under me and through me of the *single* wave that is *all* waves, the one wave flowing outward through all time:

atom, gene-light, quantum, what spins lifted in the rhythm under us, our words, *your* momentary constellation still entirely here—smile, eyes, the hand that still takes mine or rather holds itself straight out unclosing for a moment in my own—an odd suspended phrase—until it clasps; and voice—your face unfolding, gathering, this and no other, against the breaking line.

¶

Langebaan, May 14: sun down over Skaapeneiland (sp?), arched afterglow as from a large fire on the far side of the island, seagulls moiling mid-lagoon, choristers released, released—that odd insistence not just of what they are but an appeal, dissonant as from within a margin, open, sheer, between the world and themselves; from the ebb-line, silhouetted, the fret-water now black on silver, a single fisherman in orange waterproof rows out, leans back into the offing.

twilight turns the water to a granular screen the color of lit pewter: two boats remaining, and a buoy, the low island across the water to the west—each silhouetted with a presence so intense they seem to have been thrust up through the fabric of mere visibility, as from another world. Two wooden dories at anchor, swinging slightly but in place against the moving water, ride the motion as eternity rides time or time eternity, death life … mother's words to him "think of the happy times we've had"—he waist-deep in slow dying—our *making* what to say, all amateurs in grief … pushing through the fabric, sounds too, birdcalls entering the silence, through the sound of lapping water, as from the other side of silence or of audibility, the door of our comings and goings through this world

the sacred ibises fly home, they ride a swell of air up, up, then coast down in a long slide to their island roosts …

a calm hand levelling the spirit; or beckoning it out of the level?

earlier I breathed in time with the sigh and lapse of the lagoon. almost *hearing* the daylight recede. relapse.

a gull walks to the water, walking on until its weight is taken from it … Rilke's swan … others riding further out, one perched on a buoy

the near boat darkening still further,
hooded indigo lurks there, the memory of blue now
smouldering from its hull, oozing out like smoke; the water
so bright by contrast in the later twilight, more
luminous than daylight could have been. gulls carried
outward by the ebbing tide, their cries hitting the same
note so repeatedly the sound's unstoppable until the
repetitions slow to a last creak, sticking fast in silence.

Stars out, first dust of the Milky Way, Scorpio, Southern Cross, Orion's slow spreadeagled fall into the west.

—That smouldering, as of Lethe or some counter-lethe, hooded or unhooded essence, I now nervous that I'll always be in debt or leagued with its weird blue, not knowing whether I'm consoled or troubled by it, everywhere, the smoky/oiled color of whatever flares and abides within the shadow or excessive brightness of a life,

Sacks

sloe, plum, livid foison, pouring from the hull, gentian fuming; its slide and swirling prior, subsequent, following from under ... marbling, as fire burning behind alabaster, mantling, so Anchises' shade; pitch-blende; *the glowing violet*

and of *things*, the actual wooden hull, its number visible by day, SBH97BN, the orange inner rim and thwarts, the rope that disappears under the water

and of words, images, these too rise *from under*; can they be saved, can we unmoor them still charged by the long waveline ... as chosen words *do* carry the pressure (passion) and shaped residue of breath and thought ... to charge such creatures with the force of their emergence, our outcasting and the casting of all things, all names, all emanations

—[now in this space, the unseen LEOPARD of the Cedarberg's enlarged and roaming, smoke-like, maculate, half-hidden fur of flame and shade, the leopard of both worlds]—

As a living body casts a shadow, so this body-soul casts its odd lit issue past itself toward an unknown end (or origin of its own pulse breath source)(outer wall of time, expansion, *accelerating* outward to catch up with the enlarging shell or unshelled wave—*not circumscribed but circumscribing*). the haunting inner shadow-life, languid, ruinous but promising within itself another kind of light, reserve, re-served, expressed, held only as *held outwards* and issuing, *hope* ...

actinia; actinic; *actinism*—the property of radiant energy esp. in the visible and ultraviolet spectral regions by which chemical changes are produced:

lyric, sea-anemone, ghost-offering of life, of *this is how we live*. dark-lustered mineral, of twilight, of the doubled star of consolation. And if my hinge, like Yeats's truth, can't be known only embodied, then think again of passion and the Passion—Christ, Dionysus, Marsyas, Orpheus, metaphor and pharmakon, the singing head and ferry. ARDOR in *Paradiso* XIV, radiant energy in the spectral regions by which chemical changes are produced.

Dionysus and St. J the Baptist both with *leopard* skin, the flesh of resurrection, lyric pelt, the garment of both worlds. What is the force that lets me see this now?

¶

May 15: when others' words, however loved, will do no good. Though still the heart flows outward, now the anguish of the frightened voice must find its clarity past fear, unmuffled, memorable, with its hard edge of calling *not* from or out into the distance but near, near—I need the thread wound tightly around *my* finger, and unwound, the white grooves in the flesh return to an intenser red. What is the true *direction* of my words beyond foreshortened movements on the page, this furrowing tug and push off from the margin. ...

knowing that soon the thread, wound or unwound, will make no difference to your finger, or after my own death to mine; your warped rheumatic index finger against which you tied so many suture knots. ...

a floating cormorant dips down into its underwater dive, the tail splashing a small broken crown of light into the air

so little I can make of this, my finger pressing on the words, *mortal, mortal, mortal, burning, loved.*

¶

Massachusetts, July 10–11: Realizing as I copy out the pages from May, and dwell on them, something in them ferrying me, transporting, translating—actinium—transforming violet—realizing part of what was and is going on: the pressure now of what has happened between—my flying back from S. Africa to L.A. in early June, then back again for the funeral; the funeral, his face in the coffin—all as the very self's moulded and remoulded in ways not even evident in whatever I wrote down between mid-May and now—the pressure of his actual death, of his changed presence—so that now there's further meaning in the earlier pages. (that *further* may be a kind of smouldering itself?) Through language to rework the self.

Sacks

How afterwards it rained into the grave, and I lay sleepless in a small room, under a rain-beaten skylight, under the same rain—until my body also started falling inwards through itself into the earth.

In those pages, hesitant stitching, the loose working of threads without yet seeing the whole. Just as in absence of the grand schema we *can* do some near piecework that may have within it, *without our knowing*, required threads of a design. The poet's task now, despite doubt, ruined schema eg. re sacrifice, vision, transcendent order, is to surrender to the surviving impulse regardless of lack; and to do so not in the merely ironic postmod playful manner that risks too little: *submit*, the surrender is required precisely *because* of our not knowing (even when they knew it, still it called for surrender);—in fact this may link to lyric knowledge or *poetic* knowledge, which is not initially only cognitive, is more a way of embodying or investing via ardor. investing but also stripping, something re (un)clothing and revealing, something re the medium, and rhythm. And to trust you're finding or being found by truths—as pre-philosophical identification wasn't cognition though Plato tried to take its ecstasy and ritual up into the light of reason … the earlier wondering re sacrifice has some kind of response here, with other responses pressing up from further movements re joy

I'm also now pressed by slow rereading of *Paradiso*, throughout re smile, joy, and esp XIV sequence from love to its bright garment for the spirit, to ardor, to vision, to grace (the unearned light that lets us see the highest good), and back to love, all in relation to the later resurrection of the body. All this joined with my growing confidence re that glowing emergent flame which first burned as sheer uninterpreted image in mid-May, and with the tracked leopard, the half-imaginary actinic violet at Langebaan etc.; and the *smiles* throughout *Paradiso* joined now with Dad's smile and his saying *smile*—all the way back to his imagined spirit two years ago at Galisteo urging me to be more joyful, especially in what's near at hand. And how all this merging and emerging within love and ardor as the mantling flame within all incarnation.

that such ardor is itself a kind of answer, hinge, it's with the travelling single wave. it's sufficient, and within the embodied world—where now

Sacks

I'm sensing it more fully moving via Cedarberg and Langebaan and via words from—of those places to here at Merry Farm, the field uncut and golden, coreopsis, cosmos, the surviving olive, and the oaks. Having taken him into me in this and *as* this—greater ancient mind— joy/emergence/seeing the lasting and accompanying light. Has his suffering with such selfless grace, such strong retention-and-yet-giving of his spirit, forced us to recognize more fully the spirit in the flesh—a kind of passion. And how our last conversation was of love, the hardness of such love.

Wishing I could say this to him now that I'm seeing ahead as by acceleration toward a more accomplished joy—knowing there's still sorrow between—a *circum-scribing* joy

sweetness in the field, under the oaks, breeze and birdcalls rising on an unseen wave, and thread by thread the wide net of the heart is set to lift and hold the light, and then the light's the net; and then there is no net, only the pouring light

that earlier image (from last year) of his presence in the backlit face of the breaking waves, connected then to that first blessing after the wave breast and heave shoulder—*The Lord lift up his countenance upon thee, and give thee peace.* Here, in the world.

in the working with these notes, a kind of *preliminary* crushing, offering, burning and distilling out of them/myself—so that forward via hope to catch up with *Par* XIV which is also (by what providence?) the canto of accepted sacrifice: *e non er'anco del mio petto esausto / l'ardor del sacrificio, ch'io conobbi / esso litare stato accetto e fausto*—and not yet from my breast was drawn out *the ardor of the sacrifice* before I knew the prayer had been accepted and with favour.

Sacrifice not of the other, but of the self. An offering *to* the other.

Now, trying to find Yeats re the rose brings her thorn, the Absolute walks behind (?)—not finding the quote in my notebooks, reaching for *The Poems*, and the book opens first to where I'd years ago underlined

Sacks

Y's commentary re funeral poem for Parnell: "I ask if the fall of a star may not upon occasion, symbolize an accepted sacrifice."

the first stars coming out like thorns, our love within a larger will, his face, the unearned light, a mound of underglints, halo and threshing floor, the field loosely crowned

¶

July 12: And now the harder work

Laurie Sheck

1990–1991

Television sets, movie screens, scripts, news anchors, theme music, commercials, terms like "soundbite" and "spin-doctor" interest me more and more these days. In these images and ideas I see a way of focusing and exploring the world of my new poems, a world which mirrors what I have been experiencing in psychoanalysis: the disparity between the "official" story and the hidden one, the true one.

"What is hidden is more real than what is manifested"—Simone Weil

In a poem, it is not enough to tell the hidden story. The question is also how to look at the subterfuge, the cover, how power functions to block out what it can't absorb, what would undermine it.

❦

Our eyes get used to things, our ears get used to things. I was reading today about DW Griffith's early use of close-ups. Instead of showing a whole person, he would zero in on a face. We are so used to that now, we don't even think about it. But when audiences first saw it, they panicked. It looked to them like pieces of hacked up people up there on the screen, horrible, fragmented, grotesque. To examine what it is we have gotten used to, and how it has affected us, changed us. The annihilation of slow time (MTV, Sesame Street, etc) for example, what has it cost us? How has it shaped us?

❦

Henry James on skyscrapers: "monuments to the temporary": how does it affect us to live in such a world? World of weekly installments, of the "new and improved," of "updates," of the latest "in" disease.

❦

The poet unmasks the language of power. The language of power is the language of the lie.

❦

Sheck

Cocteau's limping angels. Beauty limps, he says.

How to place that wounded beauty against the backdrop of what seems so monolithic, so cold and unhurt, so horribly beyond feeling?—James's skyscrapers, the airbrushed faces in advertisements, etc. Not to isolate each from the other but to look at the interaction.

How often I think of Simone Weil. When she was 18 months old her mother tried to wean her from her bottle. The child would not eat any solid food though. The mother insisted, the child grew more and more frail. The mother consulted doctor after doctor. Finally one doctor said, "Madame, if you insist upon feeding your daughter this way she will die." The soul's refusal; its mysterious insistence on a kind of purity, its own integrity. So the child was fed thickened liquid through a bottle, and lived.

Weil knew how easy it is to take away someone's dignity, to crush them. Not hard. Easy. It is frightening how easy it is.

¶

And if Bartleby had lived? But how could he possibly have lived? And of course the story had to take place on Wall Street, enemy of the isolate mysterious hurt soul.

¶

Poetry that takes the vulnerable self, its softness and confusion, its groping, and places it up against the sheen and hardness of skyscrapers, slogans, etc. That juxtaposition. And says: now what do we have here? What comes of all this? What specific types of degradation does the soul suffer in such a context?

"The vulnerability of the precious things in life is beautiful, because vulnerability is a sign of existence."—Weil

"Purity is not invulnerable to pain, but eminently vulnerable to it … eminently vulnerable in the sense that every attack on the part of evil makes it suffer, that all evil which touches it passes into it as suffering."—Weil

¶

The light of the world we live in: neon, frenzied, traffic lights, marquee lights, ambulance light, high crime lights, television screens, their flickering, and strobe lights, headlights. This quickness.

¶

Ingeborg Bachmann: "I crawled from a womb of machines." Yes. To examine that. And how our machines have changed and are changing, growing more hushed and swifter all the time: xerox machines, fax machines, electronic surveillance devices. How this quietness ties into the language of power, of lies.

¶

If everything is to be "used," as in an extreme market economy, what place is there for beauty, for the untouched, and if there is no place, or only a marginal place, what specific types of degradation are suffered because of it? What does it mean to have a "self" in such a world?

¶

Gregor Samsa the salesman. He was USEFUL to his family; he supported them. He was obedient. He carried his salesman's sample case from town to town doing the bidding of others, bringing home the necessary money. His was a degraded soul. And it was that degraded soul that finally showed itself when he woke up one morning in the shape of a giant bug. His soul showed itself in the way that those who are not permitted genuine spoken expression come to show themselves— through the language of the body, just as the abused child who survives by consciously forgetting the abuse articulates the "forgotten" experience through bodily suffering. And of course language is dangerous, the truth is dangerous. Bodily suffering (like Gregor's transformation) the LANGUAGE of bodily suffering, of psychosomatic illness, is easily misunderstood, and therefore safer. Embodied in Gregor was the longing to be understood and the fear of being understood. The longing to make the hidden manifest, and the fear of it as well. At the core of many poems is the equivalent of Gregor Samsa—his damaged, rotting shell, the odd insect voice he does and does not recognize as his own. The self at once shown and encoded. The music and silence of that damage, and the purity that stubbornly survives that damage, as Gregor did not.

¶

Purity is the opposite of manipulation.

¶

The color of Cassandra's scream.

¶

Cassandra was most pure when she spoke not to manipulate, but when, at Agamemnon's palace, she knew she was beyond influencing anyone at all. I think she spoke then to experience her own purity before she died, to pay homage to her purity in that way; to the purity in herself and in others.

¶

Simone Weil: "The troublesome horse. He is valuable, for it is he that pulls toward the beautiful … The troublesome horse pulls toward beauty (of whatever kind it may be) in order to feed himself pleasurably thereon. He has got to be hurt until he reaches the point where he fears the beautiful instead of desiring it. At the end of this training, his energy, which was pulling toward the beautiful, now offers a resistance; but at this moment the winged principle is in the process of growth and the very itch produced by the growing wings carries one on toward the beautiful.

The resistance to be overcome in order to be carried toward the beautiful is perhaps a test of authenticity."

¶

If one had no belief in human goodness, in tenderness, or any hope for it, could one feel terror?

¶

If I am watching the 11 o'clock news and there is a person on the screen suffering, mutilated, grieving, whatever, and that person doesn't feel real to me, or only real in the most cursory and fleeting of ways, aren't I participating in the violation and degradation of that person? Poetry is subversive in that it stands in opposition to vicarious, distanced watching, to spectatorship and morbid curiosity.

¶

Pound: "Where the dead walked/ and the living were made of cardboard."

¶

If I were to really look into the children's eyes, the sufferers' eyes (How Soft this Prison is), If I were to feel them (Pain Has an Element of Blank), If I were moved by them to take some action (our stapled feet). … I was an anchorman (it was a dream, I was asleep); I looked into the teleprompter. I spoke. My voice was steady. I straightened my tie. I cracked a joke after we broke for a commercial. The commercial showed Timex watches doubling as beachchairs. The survey said viewers found it amusing. Then the signal came on, and my face came back to fill the screen.

¶

The language of television and its implications: Brought to you by (implied presence of money, corporations); Stay tuned to this same station (competition); We'll be right back (time, quickness, speed, each moment something to be filled); News that you can use (utility, immediate applicability as opposed to genuine knowledge).

¶

Last night, this dream: It is dusk. I see my hair, in waves, reflected in a large glass window. In the sky images are being projected—ghostly advertisements, filmy, but there. They appear and disappear. I find this creepy; even the sky has been taken over by technology. The full moon comes. But is it the real moon or a fake moon? It looks real, but is it just an image of the moon being projected onto the sky? I can't tell. How horrible, I think, to ruin one's belief in the moon, that one sees it, not some false image of it. Then I wake up.

¶

Oedipus and Jocasta. The question of truth and lies, of blindness and seeing, of what must be faced if one is to survive.

From Bettelheim's "Freud and Man's Soul": "Jocasta, who clearly states that she does not wish to discover the truth, cannot face it when it is revealed, and she perishes.

"Oedipus, who does face the truth, despite the immense dangers to himself of which he is at least dimly aware, survives. Oedipus suffers much, but at the end, at Colonus, he not only finds peace, but is called to the god and is transfigured."

¶

The holiness of seeing.

¶

Jocasta couldn't face, didn't want to face, her own cowardice. She was the criminal much more so than Oedipus, because she had sent her own child off to be killed shortly after its birth. She listened too easily to the oracle whom, she well knew, often spoke in riddles difficult to decipher. Yet she took the oracle at face value. That was her crime—to not protect the innocence of the newborn child who could not protect himself. To choose herself over that child. To violate innocence is to contaminate oneself; there is no purity after that. Oedipus did not violate innocence. He was, from the very beginning of his life, violated. What chance had he ever to *see*, being cut off, as he was, from the truth of who he was? The story of his life as he knew it was built on lies. Only by finally facing those lies could he be, in the end, transfigured.

※

Arno Karlen on Cocteau: "poetry is a force rather than a form."

※

Walter Pater on Leonardo da Vinci: "And because it was perfection of that style, it awoke in Leonardo some seed of discontent which lay in the secret places of his nature. For the way to perfection is through a series of disgusts … his art, if it was to be something in the world, must be weighted with more of the meaning of nature and purpose of humanity."

※

"Lad of Athens, Faithful be
To Thyself,
and Mystery—
All the rest is Perjury—"
    —Emily Dickinson.

William Stafford

1991

January 4: What moves me, what looms in my life, may not be what works in managing the material and political parts. So I learn not to depend on the innermost elements of my being, but to subordinate feelings and preferences. My success depends partly on my repression—

Even in politics, where I learn to calculate even as others do. As a result none of us clearly stands for what our most significant feelings would prefer. And the calculus results in conduct that may belie our purest feelings.

¶

January 26: I must explore the revision that happens before you write anything down.

¶

March 30: When you write you invite a reader to look in through a window on everything—and to feel, taste, hear, smell, *participate with* what is there. You can explain, but mostly you point out, part by part, and the sweep of the whole.

¶

February 4: On the plane yesterday an insight about writing: you catch at the edge of a feeling or idea or glimpse or sound—and you don't let go. You merge along with it, almost as if your hands play over it, pushing, extending, turning it over, encouraging it. And all this activity awakes other feelings, ideas, glimpses, sounds. Things get exciting; you let yourself be persuaded that a unity is possible.

¶

February 10: If you get important enough you even speak in italics. Others have to take a longer time to teach you anything, for they must contend first with your assumption that you don't need to learn.

¶

October 5 (1990): It is usual in a speech to prepare the ground, to spread out assumptions, needed context, understandings needed for a foundation of whatever is put forward. Much of this the audience may already assume, base their lives on, and understand. That redundant part of a speech irks me, and some speeches never get beyond being a reminder. A poem may skip that, silently assume it, and abruptly make use of it, twist it, subvert it, *use* it.

A poem knows where you already are, and it nails you there.

¶

January 7: If legends, myths, and stories embody even the subconscious currents of people's wants and needs, then maybe gossip in a bar carries that kind of cargo.

Sharp Ears—Now what people say clings like rain to what the words mean. A remark won't fade but grows vivid as it curves to follow a speaker and plaster itself forever on the back. I'm afraid to listen: too much of the saved-up, too much of the concentrated story, spills out of the bottle and spreads out instantly all over earth and sky.

A tremor, they say, remains, a lasting heartbeat far down inside every atom. It can't forget what happened; it carries creation's pang forever, hidden but tremendously there. And that immanence lingers in all things, ready to tremble its helpless dance again in the presence of atoms like mine.

¶

January 22: In daily life, in living, I try to be in control. I act brave. I don't shiver. I level off extremes of excitement or apathy. But in reading or attending a theater or listening to music, or entering conversations that interest me, I lean into whatever is happening. I shiver when the wind blows, hoot the villain, cower at danger, embrace what is offered. The relief of participation changes my life.

¶

Stafford

January 11: Art is a touch-and-go affair. Some things, when you learn how, you're not doing them anymore. For they are a gift; you can't demand them. You have no right, just the privilege, and it may be taken away or awarded all over again.

Kierkegaard tells how a head of lettuce, to have that succulent heart, requires time, leisure. He compares this to the meditation time, the dwelling in the inner life, that real human living requires.

※

January 20: A thought came. I did not want to write the sadness of it. Hello, Today. Let's walk awhile together. Tell me your intentions. That way, we can help each other, and maybe forget tomorrow. You be today, I'll be tomorrow.

※

February 26: On a recent trip to the East Coast I found that poets' revising goes so far as to have *others* monitor the needed changes. In effect, a committee is writing those poems. Being critics together, the writers manage to create texts that receive favorable reviews. Strange.

※

February 17: Always do your writing in the wilderness—I was thinking that sentence when I woke up yesterday.

At first the pen doesn't know where to go. It has been away for awhile and is now a little aimless. Besides, one of the world wars has begun somewhere off there beyond the horizon, making any random journey seem frivolous or even an act of treason—("What were you doing, Daddy, in that evident or more hidden war that is always going on whether you know it or not?")

So the pen, taking account of all that but unable still to do much about it, listens carefully to its own whispering and tries whatever direction the next word wants to go, meanwhile keeping in mind that sooner or later it will be necessary to spell out a meaning for all apparent meandering. (If you ever touch that real lost way you never even want to find your main path again; that's what bothers those who intend to guide you.) (What they're afraid of is, a new star shows up and all the old patterns turn into delusion and chaos.)

No wonder the pen tries to escape its past by pretending to have a future. There might be a way to escape, somewhere in the middle of things, if that awful responsibility of beginning and ending didn't haunt all who have to travel to live.

¶

April 21: About physics, apparently most of us (and maybe all of us?) can't encompass the scale and proportions involved in the realms of the very small and the very large. The realizations needed are *inconceivable*.

And maybe in the arts, too, a sense of the differences wrought by adjustments in sound, color, meaning …—this sense is unevenly distributed among people. Non-artists maybe just don't know how significant little changes are.

¶

April 15: For a superior person, it is a little harder to believe in democracy. And if you are powerful, like an editor or something, and are selecting for a magazine or for publication you are liable to think of what you reject as inferior, whereas it may just be *other*.

¶

If you think of the right questions, the answers are always being given.

If you are alert enough, every remark has a long vista.

The labyrinth you can't get out of is the one you create as you climb.

A gun can choose. A bullet has no choice.

It wasn't a place—time is where I came from.

¶

Stafford

February 3: For a long time they thought maybe there was a soul, that maybe lives had reasons, were sent from somewhere and found their way through the world and on with new duties and rewards and companions.

Maybe, in the evening when light changes and a day floods away into the horizon, that old thought comes again, settling quietly in the minds of survivors who lift their eyes from the ground and search earnestly through light, through shadow. Any friends or family who were taken away would survive somewhere in a better realm, restored, cherished, because life is precious and our joys and sorrows must have meaning.

So all your life you wonder. Sometimes a glimmering almost arrives. Your soul stirs in a gust that has come from nowhere and carries itself away, a promise of more, of revelation and rest.

Eleanor Ross Taylor

The artist moves to a new house./The excrescence of the brain is heavy/ exacts crates and webbing/old bindings suffer stress/under the idea become concrete./The stage the wooden soldiers dance on./A strange man rings a doorbell and presents/a little jar of something from his wife.

    lyric plum, partmented orange, highly organized
        pineapple

Weeks into May,
        I haven't turned my calendar.
This page shows April's frog
     about to jump.

the toad has assumed his shape
again in the night
    then they turn to dark grasses
        to frog

The dough's resting, Sarah always said.

¶

"Aren't you cute, in your little black stockings!"/I wanted to blurt out, Marigold's dead/But I couldn't embarrass her, she does care so/about finesse, and at our age some/body's always dead, black stockings, or/naked legs. *There is no discharge in that war.*

¶

DA CAPO   Life is full/of many deaths this spring./After the storm the thrush/stabbed again and again/mid-air at that spot/its nest had been/then dropped/as down a shaft/   The suckling cat/prowled loft aloud/milk-swollen, rocked,/musing at me eyes slit./   Dear Eleanor I am sorry/about your mother my mother/died fifty years ago/sometimes it seems/yesterdayYrs Allen/   Beloved little bones/   And hymn by wish bewitched/lies on, between its teeth/*His mercy faileth never*

¶

Taylor

September my fifty-fourth, 1974: "Still a lot of day left."/(But so many clouds/it seems night.)/I draw the shade.

¶

their friendship was like a planetary conjunction

destiny making its decisions, storming in the trees,
flicking at the roof all night its electric towels

    the streets of 3:30
    Do those night thoughts live in the brain?
    I can never find them by day, unless I have
    written them down, in the dark

  my battle with that luminous dial
    you're just lucky I didn't get up any earlier
    you five o'clock you

his garden followed him to the grave,
you could tell, beginning with the gate.

    Think of sitting idly by while a mouse washed its face.
I have too much of the old Diana in me to do it.

that drunk sings like a cakewalk, with one foot in the
next bar
More Rags

Scarlatti In Black
("A gentleman in black had been standing quietly in
a corner.")

    we are all adopted.

the were-rabbits celebrated defeat until there were none left

¶

"Great are the satisfactions of an industrious, well-to-do and great life, but greater still is the attraction of the abyss." —Dino Buzzati

¶

every morning he goes off to his room and builds poems, tack tack tack

    veerly veerly I sayuntoyou—the heathern—
the glory-dawn!

dream: a multi-striped casket on legs, with candles in both hands, walking away—captioned "understanding in search of its reward"

dream: of being surrounded by friends, along a counter, in a drug store. That feeling of a big fan blowing. A smell of lemons. Idleness beckoning.

dream: of being with a group walking down the middle of University Ave. in early evening going to a play. The camaraderie of youth. So alien now

dreams of houses, rooms unfolding, hallways, windows ahead, looking out through many layers, recesses

dream: a very small dog, or kitten, gray and reddish—fox-like?—trapped under a small building—an old kitchen? smokehouse?—by three big dogs on the kill, a foxhound, a lab, a boxer?—and I, exerting all my strength, reached under and pulled it out safe.

the sinewy animals that run for a living

¶

Taylor

"It is almost a definition of liberty that it shall be insecure."
—Hubert Butler

¶

(Beach Holiday)
    travelling incognito;
    incognito, not travelling

  forgotten but not gone

Jane in old galoshes—doing the sacred step
  and Diana dragging one foot

¶

Hardy's "My Team"—
  "I use a dead gal's lipstick"

    my mother in her nightgown, crying, rubbing her
      cuff under her nose
    fate never found the right word for her

somebody said his mother's life was ornamental, that she ornamented life, that was the word they used—and so it was—with things brittle and fragile, glassy and metallic, and she lived to sweep them all up

the hero's travelling-boat grows its own tarantella waves

¶

August 1989: Monteagle has become more beautiful than Sewanee, perhaps as something that doesn't have to exist does over something that exists for a purpose? Sewanee goes on for the University and the Church. Monteagle's almost junky cottages might have been abandoned, but every house is nurtured, its characteristics fostered, even the Plateau gardened with oak leaf hydrangeas, hemlocks, cleome, a profusion of hanging baskets and pots on porches. Everything kept—bridges over the ravines, Woman's Club, stone arch to the playground, the bandstand, auditorium, and gym. Tennis courts kept up. The Gate the same. The children's programs go on without better names—Eaglets, Eagles, and Ravens. The big pointed star light was on in Andrew's log cabin and his porch full as always of piled-up wood and chairs, couches, swings, dogs, and drinks and people.

¶

    (my news story)
        What—?
        Where—?
        Why—?
            They had me there

¶

"I prithee, when were we so merry? My hair tangles."
                                              —*The Duchess Of Malfi*

¶

The poem stands a long time like a ghost at the edge of the mind; gradually moves in and fills it with itself fleshed out

suddenly you find yourself enveloped by the poem, a landscape charcoaled in around you, part picture and part lines of words, the vistas not yet in organized succession, receding and advancing indecisively

(as Randall did)
(memorizing your poem to work on it)
there in its natural habitat it can grow as it prefers

(somebody painting in the dark?)

not reading your own poem in an anthology—like avoiding your face in a mirror.

Taylor

the discursive in cursive clothing

Wallace Stevens: "half prayer, half ditty"
                    ("Tea" a version of "Arrival At The Waldorf"?)

    a little tragedy with a happy ending

Don't fish for poetry in these poems—
you won't find a line

¶

"My dear Fanny....Wisdom is better than wit, and in the long run will certainly have the laugh on her side."
                                                —Jane Austen

¶

    hero-worship: the fallacy of the all-round genius

¶

dream, April 1985: A room off a bright east corridor, like the basement classrooms at NHS, or nursing home rooms. It was where Mamma was living and I was looking for her—searching—feeling anxiety and despair, regret (I had *lost* her). Looked in the walk-in closet, like our big ones in Gainesville. She was kneeling against the wall, in nearly fetal position, so withdrawn as to be almost extinguished, in a little black mound, and my heart broke. Jamie and I began patting and petting her, like soothing a baby, to try to get her to let us help her up, but she did not respond. When I picked her up there was under her black dress only a white gift box such as dresses come in, and the old black fringed wool scarf she wore over her head when she went outdoors those last years, and two or three trinkets and bits of bric-a-brac. I felt *she* must be somewhere. Dr. Galen [Columbus, Ohio] looked in and I said, Doctor I can't find her. On a desk/table was a pile of bright red-and-gold pictures—picture postcards—to her from Jean. They were of Byzantine churches and the messages were all typed travel notes. I sobbed. She had been unable to get any help for loneliness from our long-distance communications. Waked crying bitterly.

※

Reading them over again/she became once more/the hare in the trap/the bird caught in the briars/twisting and turning/towards desperate life-light-speech/(How did, I get out?)/leaving a feather—/a bit of fur—a foot/ (several feet!)

※

"Y'all men-folks better watch out. We women-folks'll *sho* trip you up every time!"—heard on NPR, street interview about Mayor Barry

※

LOLLING IN THE DECK CHAIR   I wouldn't run hell for leather/around that oak limb/away up there/not for a million dollars./ Especially at that speed./Especially after another squirrel

※

May 9, 1986: a long dream about a baby—adopted, I thought. As in many of my dreams about babies, it was grotesque—not really a baby. What did it represent? It was very tiny, in fluffy dress and cap, and I was very happy in my care of it. I felt my relationship with it keenly—and that it was an especially dear baby. I was busy with a lot of things, but felt I was going to keep *this* baby always with me, not off in its room for naps, with babysitters, etc. Suddenly I realized it was missing (often in my dreams I've mislaid, forgotten, neglected the baby) and saw that a young couple had been sitting on it. It was wrapped in a piece of clear plastic and had turned into a flattish, blue, fetus-like object—I thought of a frog run over on the highway. I seized it, held it to my face and breathed into its little face (rather like a porcupine's) under its cap. I blamed myself for not knowing resuscitation procedure, but it began turning pink and fleshing out, then began breathing. I kept blowing into its face a while, put it down and hurried away to get some milk.

I first thought these dreams of a baby were about my mother, and that they began with my anxiety for her care. Sometimes I think they could be about my writing. Perhaps, as Loulie Cocke suggested, they are simply about my own children.

❡

"I was requested not to speak, as a feast was about to be given to the dead, whose spirits delight in uninterrupted silence."
—Indian captive

❡

"… an Egyptian desert snail (Helis desertorum) on the assumption that the shell was empty, was fixed to a card in the British Museum in March 1846; in March 1850, traces of slime were noted on the tablet, which was immediately immersed in water, when presently the shell became detached from the card and the animal began to crawl about."
—Encyclopedia Britannica

Rosanna Warren

1990

August: Vermont. From his study: A single dry beech leaf hangs from a branch of balsam by a spider web strand. I saw the same leaf last August, is it possible it has survived a winter of blizzards when a man has died?

Pond water glints through pine boughs. The mind of the forest: years and years of layered decaying leaves.

You brought me a small gray stone. I showed you an empty palm. To write the icon, slide cloudlight over the surface of the pond. It will adhere. We will read it together, years from now.

¶

Tightening noose of a November afternoon. Sex on my fingers, honey from Mt. Hymettos on our thighs. I love this hour of erasure, this season stripping down in chill rain and gray. The trees are divested, the suburban lawns are numb, the twigs
and vestiges are cast down,
And whatever small knowledge remains
Is to be cherished in the spine, the wrist pulse, the primitive *mons* which guards its secret against and into the circling down of night, the wheeze and shush of distant, hurrying tires.

¶

from Marcel Schwob, *Le Livre de Monelle* (1895):
>"Don't wait for death: she is with you. Be her companion and hold her close: she resembles you.
>
>Die your own death; don't envy the deaths of ages past …"
>
>"Burn the dead carefully, and scatter their ashes to the four winds of heaven …"
>
>"Bequeath yourself nothing, neither pleasure nor sorrow."
>
>"And she said, from afar: Forget me and I will be returned to you."

¶

Warren

Dragging my innocence over the surface of the earth like a chain.

※

My spine a braid of pain.

※

Buber: "All real living is meeting."

※

W.S., from "An Ordinary Evening in New Haven":

XXIII

>In this identity, disembodiments
>
>Still keep occurring. What is, uncertainly,
>Desire prolongs its adventure to create
>Forms of farewell, furtive among green ferns.

XXXI

>…Like an evening evoking the spectrum of violet,
>A philosopher practicing scales on his piano,
>A woman writing a note and tearing it up.
>
>It is not in the premise that reality
>Is a solid. It may be a shade that traverses
>A dust, a force that traverses a shade."

※

Chiara, aged four, on Pierre from her day care: "Is he French, or a human being?"

To me, the other day, objecting to my reading aloud: "I *hate* it when you rhyme! Your mouth goes all wibble wobble and you look like a cow."

Later: "Drawing-writing is stronger than word-writing."

※

Warren

The father, in whom disease is chewing at lungs, brain, liver, and lymph glands, arrives to collect his young daughter from an afternoon of play at our house. He is thin, he wears a baseball cap and sunglasses. "How are you?" he asks cheerfully. "Fine, thanks," I reply, and in order not to ask him how he is, declare, with obtuse heartiness, "They played well this afternoon, they had a wonderful time." "Good, good," he says. His daughter, who does not know what is in store for them, gallops up: "Daddy!" He leans to embrace her, her arm is soft around his neck, her light hair falls over his shoulder.

¶

Biography: a low mimetic mode. Precisely. By any means. So let it lead me. "We are saved by what we cannot imagine." (Ashbery).(Are we saved?) Give me your hand.

SENECA REVIEW

Deborah Tall, Editor
Hobart & William Smith Colleges
Geneva, New York 14456

Available Back Issues
$5.00 each

Vol. XIII, No. 2. Feature: Poems and an interview with English poet Andrew Harvey. Poems by Heather McHugh, David St. John, Stephen Dunn, Ann Lauterbach, Hilda Morley, and others. Essays by Dave Smith and Jonathan Holden.

Vol. XIV, No. 1. Translations of Rilke, Akhmatova, and from classical and contemporary Arabic poetry. Poems by Rosanna Warren, Carol Frost, Jane Kenyon, Eric Pankey, Walter McDonald, Luis Omar Salinas, Geraldine C. Little, and others.

Vol. XIV, No. 2. Feature: Poems and an interview with Stephen Dunn. Poems by Christopher Buckley, Linda Gregerson, Laurie Sheck, Debra Nystrom, Michael J. Rosen, and others. Essays on Ellen Bryant Voigt and Charles Wright.

Vol. XV, No. 1. Arrowsmith translations of Montale. Levitin translations from the Portuguese. Poems by Charles Simic, Stephen Dobyns, Peter Sacks, Maura Stanton, Myra Sklarew, Gary Soto, Elizabeth Spires, Susan Stewart, Jordan Smith, Albert Goldbarth, Judith Kitchen, and others.

Vol. XV, No. 2. Guest-edited by Stephen Dobyns. Poems and an interview with Thomas Lux. Poems by Ellen Bryant Voigt, C.K. Williams, Ray Carver, Bill Knott, Steve Orlen, Mary Karr, and others.

Vol. XVI, No. 1. Special International Issue. Poems from the Catalan lands, the Middle East, and Asia. Irish poet Eavan Boland.

Vol. XVI, No. 2. Feature: Poems and an interview with David St. John. Merwin translations of Roberto Juarroz. Poems by Seamus Heaney, Rita Dove, Jared Carter, Susan Stewart, William Heyen, Patricia Goedicke, David Wojahn, and others.

Vol. XVII, No. 1. Poems by Gregory Orr, Mekeel McBride, Donald Finkel, Cleopatra Mathis, T. Alan Broughton, and others. Eight Upstate New York Writers. Translations from South America. Mary Karr on "Missing Larkin"

Vol. XVIII, No. 1. Poems by Robert Pack, Carl Dennis, Molly Peacock, James Reiss, Maurya Simon, Barbara Goldberg, and others. An essay by Stephen Kuusisto on Japanese poet Nanao Sakaki.

Vol. XVIII, No. 2. Poems by Cornelius Eady, Robert Farnsworth, Brooks Haxton, Richard Frost, C.S. Giscombe, and others. Translations from the Bengali and Japanese.

Vol. XIX, No. 1. Poems by Hayden Carruth, William Matthews, Patricia Goedicke, T. Alan Broughton, Sharon Bryan, and others. Translations of Yannis Ritsos, Raúl Barrientos, and Galician-Portuguese Troubadour Poetry.

Vol. XIX, No. 2. Feature: Contemporary Polish Poetry—an interview with Stanislaw Baranczak and a selection of poems translated by him and Clare Cavanagh. Poems by Denise Levertov, Cornelius Eady, Vern Rutsala, Diane Glancy, Gerald Early, Carol Frost, and others. Translations of Jules Supervielle, Max Jacob, Angel Gonzalez, and Mihai Eminescu by Geoffrey Gardner, Rosanna Warren, Steven Ford Brown, Pedro Gutirrez Revuelta, and W.D. Snodgrass.

Vol. XX, No. 1. **Special twentieth anniversary issue.** *In the Act: Essays on the Poetry of Hayden Carruth*, guest-edited by David Weiss. Essays by Wendell Berry, Philip Booth, David Budbill, W.S. Di Piero, Geoffrey Gardner, Sam Hamill, Geof Hewitt, Carolyn Kizer, Maxine Kumin, Stephen Kuusisto, William Matthews, David

Rivard, Anthony Robbins, and David Weiss. And an interview with and new poems by Hayden Carruth. Available for $6.95.

Vol. XX, No. 2. Poems by Eleanor Ross Taylor, Mekeel McBride, Liz Rosenberg, David Baker, Marilyn Chin, and others. Translations of Ritsos, Moreno, Vaiciunaite, and de Andrade. Essay by Stephen Dunn: "Alert Lovers, Hidden Sides, & Ice Travelers: Notes on Poetic Form & Energy."

Vol. XXI, No. 1. Poems by Robert Pack, T. Alan Broughton, Mekeel McBride, Linda McCarriston, William Dickey, and others. Translations of Martial, and from the Yiddish, Hungarian, and Polish. Stephen Kuusisto on "Robert Bly's *Iron John* and the New 'Lawrentian' Man."

Enter my subscription for_____year(s). (Rates: $8/year; $15/2 years. *Seneca Review* is published twice yearly, spring and fall.)

Send the following back issues for $5.00 each: _____

(40% discount to bookstores.)

Make check payable to *Seneca Review,* and mail orders to Deborah Tall, Editor, *Seneca Review,* Hobart & William Smith Colleges, Geneva, NY 14456.

Name _____

Address _____

_____

ANNOUNCING
A SECOND CHANCE AT TWO DECADES
In case you missed them the first time around

Hobart and William Smith Colleges Press, publisher of *Seneca Review*, proudly announces the complete reprinting of *The Fifties* and *The Sixties*, that dramatic and influential magazine edited by Robert Bly. Shot from the original editions, the entire ten issues have been reprinted in unmodified facsimile form. If you missed the fireworks the first time around, don't miss them this time!

> How marvelous to read again these issues of *The Fifties* and *The Sixties*. With humor, crankiness, and plain good sense, this magazine tilted its lance at what it saw as the tired conventions of American poetry.... One can only applaud the Hobart and William Smith Colleges Press in this timely enterprise.
> —David St. John

For more information and orders, write to:
H & WS PRESS
Hobart & William Smith Colleges
Geneva, New York 14456
$5.95 each, or $40 for the entire set of 10.